JUMPIN

1st Edition

Published in 2012 by
Woodfield Publishing Ltd
Bognor Regis PO21 5EL England
www.woodfieldpublishing.co.uk

ISBN 1-84683-132-6

Printed and bound in England

Cover design by Mike Rowland

Jumping Beans

*Personal reminiscences of an
'oddball' Royal Air Force Unit – No.1
Parachute Training School (PTS)*

EDWARD CARTNER

Woodfield

Woodfield Publishing Ltd

Bognor Regis ~ West Sussex ~ England ~ PO21 5EL
tel 01243 821234 ~ **e/m** info@woodfieldpublishing.co.uk

Interesting and informative books on a variety of subjects

For full details of all our published titles, visit our website at
www.woodfieldpublishing.co.uk

Also by Edward Cartner

Non-Fiction
Glancing Blows
I Have Control
Who Is In Charge Here?
Parachutes Princes & Predicaments
Carry On Corporal

Fiction
Sweet & Sour

The PTS badge.

~ CONTENTS ~

Preface

'Knowledge Dispels Fear' is the apposite motto of the Royal Air Force No 1 Parachute Training School (PTS). Like many military slogans it proclaims a succinct hint of the unit's function; yet this one might be reversed under the stress of terrifying, first-time experience.

In 2009 Peter Hearn, President of the veteran parachute jumping instructors' Canopy Club, invited me to produce 'some form of memorial booklet, perhaps outlining the history of PTS in anecdotal form'. The project, intended as a members'-only piece, came to fruition in 2010 and went some way towards marking the 70th anniversary of the Parachute School, together with the 65th of the Club.

In this work I aim to develop the theme and to reflect on the life and work of PTS and on the deeds of those specialised parachute jumping instructors (PJIs) who served there, and at other places employing the same skills. My musings will cover around 50 years: 1940 being the school's beginning; 1989 being the year of my last parachute jump and 1993 marking the end of my contact as a uniformed serviceman.

In the latter part of my own service and into retirement I came to puzzle over why it was that the existence of PTS, its people and their work is barely acknowledged in supposedly authoritative accounts of the Service. Was it because throughout its history the school's primary purpose has been to the Army? In that, did the unit fall invisibly between RAF flying training and ground training philosophy?

Whatever the reason, it is an indisputable fact that PJIs have served in war and peace from Indonesia to California, from Arctic Norway to the South Atlantic, and continue so to do. Of course, there have been written accounts, but nothing that could be called an official history.

I make no claim to attempt that now – I am neither historian nor archivist – but individual PJIs have added to my 'story bank' – verbal and written – over a period of many years and with their permission I can withdraw from a strong deposit account. It is these that evoke my own memories and which may tell the story of No 1 Parachute Training School. The reader may be surprised by the scope of the unit's work.

This is not a history book: my account is too personal, erratic in its chronology and relies heavily on anecdotal evidence. In many places it may not even record accurately the 'facts' – memory is a fickle tool – but despite these failings I hope to capture the essential spirit of a unique RAF unit. It is a place of mischievous humour, professional optimism and surprising modesty: one whose people have a high regard for No 1 Parachute Training School, the Airborne Brotherhood and their own mysterious trade.

The school, of course, still exists, but others will have to bring matters up to date. Of course, what is told in here in no way whatever reflects the view of Her Majesty's Government, the Royal Air Force or even No 1 Parachute Training School.

Edward Cartner, May 2012

About The Author

Edward Cartner was commissioned into the Royal Air Force in May 1964 and retired in August 1993.

Between other duties during that time he served in eight different appointments at No 1 Parachute Training School Royal Air Force, including three with the British Army's Airborne Forces.

This is his fifth book for Woodfield about RAF life.

PTS insignia, as worn on working and dress uniforms.

1.   THE BEGINNINGS – WHAT

History tells us that Winston Churchill was a feisty character, a forceful wartime leader wont to issue abrupt demands for 'Action This Day'. The military chiefs would be summonsed to receive instructions on the latest strategic thinking; how they effected the requirements was, of course for them to puzzle over.

Thus were the various beginnings made and for British military parachuting the record shows that the seeds were sewn in Churchill's note of June 1940:

"We ought to have a corps of at least five thousand parachute troops. Pray let me have a note from the War Office on the subject."

No doubt the War Office staffs had enough on their plate than to dream up a whole new way of going to war. There is more than one suggestion from those days that the notion of dropping fighting troops from the air and behind the enemy's guard was in some ill-defined way, *just not cricket, don't you know.* Such reaction was probably from the same mind-set that averred, *Tanks will never replace horses*; a view that appears frequently in British and other military mythology.

Nonetheless, Churchill had spoken, and in any case there were a few comparisons to be drawn: By 1940 the German army had demonstrated an advanced parachute assault capability. They had learned from the Russians who had been developing airborne delivery systems since the late 1920s.

So, what to do? How to form this parachute force? Of military parachuting there was no practical knowledge, no equipment and in some quarters little meaningful support. There was, however, a pool of men who had done some parachute jumps, sometimes as an adjunct to their normal duties, and after Churchill's announcement these were to form the first band of instructors.

Dennis (Danny) Gavin was one of these. Nearly 70 years later he wrote of those days:

... little or nothing is known about how mass parachute jumping was perfected by the RAF Parachute Jumping Team located at RAF Henlow in Bedfordshire. This team of instructors were all young men willing to accept the unknown dangers of parachute jumping in order to get the Army to any battlefield ... The then conventional parachute was of little use for mass jumping. A parachute which did not require manual release was needed. A new design was produced with a static line attached to the aircraft and the pack containing the parachute.

When the parachutist jumped, the parachute would be pulled from the pack and the man would float gently to the ground with the pack and static line remaining attached to the aircraft. This new type of parachute [manufactured by the Gregory Quilter Company of Woking in Surrey] was tested by the RAF Jumping Team and finally accepted for mass jumping.

Today one can only speculate on how exactly Danny was 'picked up' by the Service to be a part of the new training team, but he does describe at some length the primitive ways – most alarming to my generation – in which parachutists were carried in and then expected to quit the aircraft in the days immediately before the Second World War:

The Vickers Virginia was known as a heavy night bomber which travelled at less than 100 miles per hour with a four man crew accommodated in open cockpits ... the framework, wings, etc. of the "Ginny" were covered with Irish linen strengthened using a dope-type paint. 1937-1938 saw the Vickers Virginia put to use for parachute testing at RAF Henlow.

For parachute jumping a platform was built on each wing behind the strut. The parachutist would stand on this platform, one on each wing, standing with his back to the slipstream...

The aircraft would take off and once over the area for the jump to be made a crew member located in the front open cockpit would signal by the wave of his arm for the parachutist to reverse his position and face the slip steam [and let go of the strut]

... the parachutist would float to the ground to the cheers of his colleagues ...This method of parachute jumping continued for some time and was carried out by the young airmen who eventually became the very first parachutist instructors...

Needless to say, dropping possibly two men at a time from the wings of a biplane was not going to meet even the embryonic requirements for airborne assault of the day and Danny Gavin's account continued by describing the latest state-of-the-art:

... the thrill and excitement of making a parachute jump from the wing of the old Vickers Virginia was never quite repeated

from the hole in the middle of its replacement aircraft, the Whitley Bomber.

Once a decision was made for parachute training to commence, a Whitley Bomber arrived at Henlow, which had to be modified with the following adjustments:-

(a) A jumping exit was created on the aircraft within the fuselage.

(b) A shield was installed on the jumping exit to protect the jumper from the effects of the slip-streams from the plane's engines.

(c) A jumping warning light was installed.

(d) A connection within the jumping exit was made to which the parachutist and his parachute were attached.

By summer 1940 a Parachute Training Centre had been established at Manchester Corporation's airport at Ringway. Maurice Newnham, who commanded the Centre – later to become PTS – for much of the War, described those early days.

'Press On Regardless' probably best describes the mood of those appointed to this mysterious new world and Newnham himself followed Louis Strange, who had been tasked to set in motion the training system. Newnham introduces Strange:

Pilot Officer Louis Strange DSO, MC, DFC – sometime Lieutenant Colonel and ace pilot in the old Royal Flying Corps – peacetime aviator and now but recently returned from active service in France ...

Throughout my own association with PTS, a large charcoal portrait of Strange, together with that of Major John Rock, adorned the PTS HQ's corridors. Strange and Rock, shortly followed by Newnham, were the true fathers of British military parachute training.

They had to fight through several degrees of inertia, not to mention continued RAF scepticism. The extraordinary facet of them all for later generations coming to PTS as newcomers was that they knew nothing about parachuting; Newnham, like Strange was a decorated pilot from the Great War in his early forties.

Nonetheless, they quickly gathered enthusiasm and equipment about them and learned on the job. Inter-service politics were overcome and despite continued RAF reluctance, it became the responsibility of that service to introduce to the Army the new transport system.

Maurice Newnham recorded one typical Air Ministry reaction:

It is the duty of the RAF to remain in the air and not to fall out of it.

No doubt the staffs had a point to make: what became known as the Battle of Britain was imminent; a defeated army had only recently been evacuated from Dunkirk; equipment and aircraft shortages were apparent everywhere, but despite all that here was an attempt to form an entirely new arm. A senior RAF staff officer summarised the problem:

There are very real difficulties in this parachute business. We are trying to do what we have never been able to do hitherto, namely introduce a completely new arm into the Service at about five minute's notice and with totally inadequate resources and personnel ... it will be necessary to cover in six months the ground that the Germans have covered in six years.

I like to think that the 'Press-on' spirit of PTS, very evident throughout my time as a PJI, was born from that despair. The anguish mattered little, as Peter Hearn, a PJI of the late 1950s generation and one-time PTS Commanding Officer, observed:

Winston Churchill had spoken.

Meanwhile the personnel were being gathered. Danny Gavin, the fabric worker at Henlow, recorded:

Mass jumping continued at Henlow until the sequence of exit from the modified Whitley was perfected. Eventually, it was decided that mass jumping was, indeed, a success and should be brought speedily into use by the British Army. The entire Henlow unit was transferred to Ringway in Manchester which, at the time, was being used as a small civil airport. Conveniently, Ringway was just a short flying distance from Tatton Park in Cheshire [which became the training dropping zone] ...

Willie Hunter, who had set off to join the Merchant Navy, got sidetracked into the RAF and after some adventurous flying in the early stages of the war reported as a trainee RAF PTI:

I attended a PT re-qualifying course in 1941 ... [then at Ringway] ... interviewed by Flt Lt Kilkenny who thought I was the first F/Sgt to apply for the job as a PJI. (Came away somewhat confused.)

The night balloon jumping through the hole, make a bad exit and you got a bloody nose. The silence was time-consuming and I thought the canopy would never open ... Experimental water drops in the lake at Tatton Park ... The unfortunate death of the trainee paratrooper whose canopy caught on the tail wheel of a Whitley ...

Willie's account introduces us to what became the only source of volunteer PJIs – the RAF Physical Training Instructor.

After 12 months of early work at PTS (at first a division of the Central Landing Establishment) the task had grown considerably and developed sufficiently into a recognisable teaching one in the hands of the RAF. Maurice Newnham persuaded his masters that the existing RAF Physical Fitness Branch would best be able to provide experienced teachers and instructors to train as PJIs. He recorded his convincing case:

'And where do you suppose we're going to find these teachers as you call them?' [his CO demanded] 'You know quite well that when we started this business twelve months ago there was no such thing as parachute training and what progress has been made has been made here. I can assure you that there is no magic pool of parachute instructors ... so don't expect me to produce them out of a hat.' ... 'No, sir [Newnham went on] But if you will get me the right men I can train them. The RAF Physical Fitness Branch has just the type. It has been tremendously expanded during the war, most of the officers and men are civilians joined up for the emergency and a lot of them are teachers by profession ...

This early plea quickly developed into an argument that was supported by the then Physical Fitness Branch of the Air Ministry and which in turn became official policy. Maurice Newnham records that on 1st November 1941:

... the Parachute Training School should become an entirely RAF unit ... Future instructors would be recruited from the Physical Fitness Branch of the RAF.

This manning policy has been in place ever since, even though it has frequently divided opinion within the branch at 'grassroots' level. Throughout my service there was always a feeling that PJIs, by taking that specialised track, had somehow divorced themselves from the profession of physical education and training. Occasionally, and it was not always bar-room banter, one would be reminded of a resentment amongst the non-PJIs over PJIs' extra pay – a fact of life – and enhanced promotion prospects. This latter was never proved, of course, but the usual PJI answer to the disgruntled could be:

Well, come and join us, it's a voluntary activity, and we're worth more to the Air Force.

By the 1960s it was common for a PJI-qualified NCO to spend almost the whole of his subsequent career on PJI duties across the gamut of PTS activity.

And so the beginnings had been made, tentative policies had been confirmed, equipment was being developed and training methods refined. In April 1941 a 'trial-run' had been attempted when a small force jumped into northern Italy to disable an important aqueduct. The damage caused was light, and all the party was captured, but the psychological impact of the new style of warfare, both on the British and the enemy, must have been considerable.

In April 1941 Churchill visited Ringway to see for himself what progress had been made. A demonstration drop was arranged: five modified Whitley bomber aircraft were to drop eight parachutists each together with some equipment containers. It was a gusty day and Maurice Newnham recalled the anxiety amongst the Prime Minister's party: a possible approach by German aircraft adding to the *frisson*:

"Hello, formation leader ... Are you ready to take off? Over ..."

"No, I'm not ready ... five of the blighters have fainted!"

As the old aircraft eventually lumbered into the air and prepared to run in for the drop:

Louis Strange and John Rock expressed their views, their confidence and difficulties ...

The Prime Minister was sympathetic, but had to confirm his strategic judgement on the demonstration given by five decrepit aircraft, which were unsuitable for the job anyway and forty parachutists of whom six failed to jump. The total fighting strength on that day was less than 400 partly-trained airborne soldiers.

Danny Gavin also recalled an early demonstration on which he was a parachutist:

A display by the five RAF parachute instructors impressed the attending military High Command and, unbeknown to the team of instructors, the display was also witnessed by the then Prime Minister, Winston Churchill, who, for security reasons, watched the display from a nearby copse. Winston Churchill asked to the introduced to the members of display team and, when shaking their hand, told each one of them he had witnessed the "birth" of the Parachute Regiment and congratulated each one of them for all their hard work and the results they had achieved in such a short time.

Massed parachutists descending from the sky can be an awesome sight to any spectator – guaranteed to halt traffic – and perhaps more so in those early days. Sixty seven years after Ringway I met a retired dentist with strong boyhood memories of watching parachutists descending over the aerodrome. Had they been, I wondered, jumping for Churchill?

2. THE BEGINNINGS – HOW

By May 1941 Louis Strange, it seems, had clearly demonstrated – to the RAF appointers at least – that he had an eye for out-of-the-ordinary 'oddball' schemes. Having overcome the initial chaotic inertia and scepticism associated with the new parachute training system his reward was to be appointed to Speke, Liverpool to oversee the development of catapult launching systems off merchant ships of fighter aircraft.

At Ringway he left a powerful legacy of 'can-do' together with a belief by all who followed that military parachuting was entirely feasible and that effective training systems could be developed to minimise the risks. This philosophy was very evident throughout my service: frequently beset by marginal weather conditions the willingness of the PJIs to complete a training parachute programme was humbling.

Meanwhile Maurice Newnham had been sent to Ringway in October 1940 as an administrative officer and recalled his appointment interview by his prospective new CO:

We're going to train soldiers to parachute ... frightfully hush-hush of course. I want an officer to start some files, look after the correspondence and generally keep things in order ... there may be a big future – I don't know ...

As things have turned out there was indeed a future to military parachuting, and it certainly became 'big' during the war.

Inevitably, there was also a 'future' for admin matters too. Maurice Newnham might well have been the first PTS administrator, but the job requirement persists to this day. Despite the robust practical 'hands-on' nature of the unit, orders, training manuals, procedures and personnel management doubtless played as big a part in his daily duties as they did in mine. I inherited his administrative role 44 years later – to be known as Chief Instructor (neither the chief, nor an instructor). I began as a PJI and became an administrator. Maurice Newnham, a 43-year old Great War aviator, began as an administrator, became a parachutist and took the newly-named Parachute Training School onwards throughout the war.

Like Louis Strange and John Rock, Newnham's portrait also graced - it still does – the PTS HQ of my time. Properly dressed in collar and tie a determined-looking man gazed steadily at everybody. On his 'battledress' blouse can be seen pilot's 'wings' and many medal ribbons. On top of everything is the all-enclosing parachute harness of the day; a secure system that was to be almost unchanged until the late 1980s.

The argument to employ physical educators as parachute instructors had been won, but there had been, of course, an embryonic staff at Ringway throughout. The original fabric workers from Henlow had been joined by experienced para-chutists who had for some years demonstrated at public air days.

There was, however, little standardised system and as the numbers of trainees grew, so did the injury rate with the occa-sional fatal accident. The pre-war professionals had prepared for landing by twisting themselves under the parachute when approaching the ground. To train large numbers of non-gymnastic soldiers in such techniques was not considered possible, so a safe landing technique had to be developed.

Much of the credit for the 'folding into the ground' landing technique used by parachutists under plain round parachutes is given to John Kilkenny.

John Kilkenny – 'JCK' in PTS mythology – joined PTS in October 1941 as 'a games player of renown and a physical education expert'. Maurice Newnham briefed him in his new role in typically robust military style:

... the work of the School was to teach soldiers to parachute without hurting themselves ... [the school] was shortly to become exclusively RAF ... the RAF had to form a properly organised parachute school in double quick time.

'But what's this to do with me ... I know nothing about parachuting – I've never jumped and I don't think that I want to.'

That's all right [Maurice replied] neither did I, but you'll soon get used to it. .

Kilkenny was to devise and supervise a ground training regime biased towards 'showing the chaps how to tumble without getting hurt'.

People have all sorts of ideas about it [Newnham continued]. Some think it's like skiing ... like jumping backwards off the top floor of a double-deckker bus travelling at twenty miles an hour. The only thing about which I'm certain at the moment is that you hit the ground with a hell of a bang ...

Certainly by the early 1960s little in that had changed, except that PTS had perfected the parachute landing roll. Parachutists landing under plain round canopies could still 'clatter in' – speaking from painful experience – despite good anticipation and agility. (By the late-1980s, however, a ram-air military 'square' parachute was available to all. Once landing this thing had been mastered – rather like a glider – 'stepping onto the ground' as if off a kerb became commonplace.)

A reliable parachute deployment system had been developed, whereby the parachutist attached a line to the aircraft, jumped out and as he fell away the backpack containing the canopy and rigging lines was pulled away from light ties thus allowing the thing to open.

Getting out of the aircraft was another problem. Standing on the wing clutching struts was not really an option, nor was edging down a narrow fuselage to be pulled off a platform in the rear turret compartment. The Army needed as many troops coming down simultaneously in one area as possible and with little scatter.

An early solution was to cut a hole in the aircraft floor and have the parachutists leave in quick order according to a choreography regulated by the despatching PJI. The aperture resembled a large dustbin set flush with the floor and was only just wide enough to accommodate a man and his bulky parachute back pack. An exaggerated position of military attention had to be adopted to permit passage when failure to do so could tilt the face forward into a painful collision with the opposite edge. 'Ringing the bell' was the fond name given to that event and still mentioned with some glee by older PJIs in the mid-1960s when I joined PTS. How they avoided such mishaps from a sitting position was an agility my generation would rather not practice. Even so, because we had an aircraft still with a floor aperture 'jumping through the hole' was part of the training, the difference being that our 'hole' allowed a full-stretch dive without ringing anything.

Many of the problems that can arise when parachuting from aircraft come from slipstream effect, especially if the parachutist is still attached, however briefly, to the machine as he falls away. During the Great War Louis Strange had probably seen 'survival' parachute jumps from doomed observer balloons and in an inspired piece of lateral thinking discussed using balloons as a parachute training aid.

Suspended under what resembled an anti-aircraft barrage balloon of the period a rickety box holding four or five trainees and an instructor was carried aloft. The silence, delayed opening of the parachute and 'cold-blooded' nature of the process was enough to give an 'additional thrill', but it did provide a cheaper and perhaps more reliable jumping platform for 'first-timers'. Balloons continued as a basic training aid at PTS well into the 1990s, as did their reputation for being the most feared of all the PTS experiences. It was not unknown in post-war years for quite well-experienced aircraft parachutists to avoid at all costs jumping from balloons; especially at night.

Maurice Newnham:

I thought that "an additional thrill" [delayed parachute opening] was putting it rather mildly. When the first balloon came to be installed at Tatton Park [the training Drop Zone nearby to Ringway] in April 1941 and men who had been trained to jump from aircraft were asked to jump from it they considered that it was a much more frightening experience. They told the most harrowing stories which literally damned it before a proper trial had been carried out ...

Late 1941, the first weeks of PTS as an RAF unit, saw the establishment of a recognisable structure to the training. Kilkenny had formalised the ground training with Harry Ward, a pre-war professional parachutist in charge of the actual jumping.

And his parachute landing roll was in use:

... a controlled collapsing fall to right or left in such a way that the forces of the impact would be taken by those parts of the body best capable of receiving It ...

This technique for landing under simple parachutes is unchanged to this day.

Similarly, the ratio of instructors to trainees and the course length was determined. Maurice Newnham recorded:

... In this respect the matter was more or less arbitrarily decided by the carrying capacity of the aircraft, and the military set-up for parachute units had already been based on this factor. As the Whitley and Wellington were the only types at that time which appeared at all likely to be available for paratroop work and their maximum load was ten men that was the strength of the smallest military unit ...

Thus ten men to one PJI became the norm – in my time usually eight to one – a ratio that by and large survived until the late 1980s and in many ways became the foundation for PTS's safety record.

The course length at Ringway had been set at a fortnight during which approximately 250 men would make seven parachute descents. Clearly, the pressures of war forced such rapid progress, but it set the scene for the enduring PTS ethos of overcoming many odds: poor weather, lack of aircraft, etc so that by the mid-1970s with a much smaller airborne army the school was still accommodating each month three 8-jump courses of 60 men each.

3.   ONWARDS FROM RINGWAY

Driven by the imperatives of conflict, Churchill's requirement – 'we ought to have a corps of at least five thousand parachute troops' – had been more than amply met by the end of World War Two.

At war's end there were two British Airborne Divisions and PTS had played a major part at Ringway in their formation. There had also been separate parachute training schools – staffed by RAF PJIs – established overseas, notably at Chaklala in India. PJIs had also flown on all the major parachute assaults such as Arnhem and the Rhine Crossing and also as despatchers on less well publicised covert operations that frequently involved long, lonely flights for perhaps only a couple of parachutists. Similarly, as Bill Jevons noted:

PTS missionaries had travelled far and wide preaching the gospel of safe parachuting ... When the story of the Burma front is written, there will be many references to the help given by PTS to the 14th Army and the Chindits. Another party of instructors [PJIs] went out to train paratroops in Egypt and Palestine and they have made many perilous trips over the mountains into Yugoslavia ...

Lieutenant General Sir Richard Gale, who had led the British 6th Airborne Division into action on 'D' Day, was unstinting in his praise:

To all who qualified and subsequently fought as parachutists the happiest memories are associated with this great school ... no less than four hundred thousand live descents by parachute were made during the war and no less than sixty thousand British and Allied parachutists were trained. The spirit that has animated so many of them to perform such grand and courageous tasks was largely laid at the Parachute Training School ...

A strong bond between the Paras and the PJIs at 'shop-floor level' had been formed and this trust became perhaps one of the most durable legacies of the wartime PTS. The troops looked for the parachute brevet amongst the aircrew, and no amount of feigned casual indifference could entirely conceal their faith in the PJIs' professionalism. They knew the RAF men weren't tough soldiers, but in the back of a crowded aircraft on a low-level rush to a night drop zone, nor perhaps were they. One crisis at a time had to be the motto, and the immediate one was to remain reassuringly in the hands of the PJI until the moment of leaving the aircraft. Meanwhile every parachutist was treated dispassionately alike: 100% attention regardless of rank or experience.

In early 1946 Ringway aerodrome was returned to civilian use and PTS was re-deployed to Upper Heyford, 10 miles or so north of Oxford. The records suggest that while there remained some disquiet that an RAF unit should be responsible for the initial training of all British parachute troops, PTS was destined carry that role into peacetime and for as long as the Army retained airborne forces. The politicians, both civilian and military, may well agonise who was going to 'pay for it all', and why should a form of training almost exclusively for the Army (and soon many Royal Marines) be an Air Force matter, but PTS remained pragmatic: it's our job; we've been doing it from the start; so it will be the best.

During this time there was, of course, mass demobilisation but many individuals opted to stay in the Service. A number of these, wholly or part-trained as aircrew, were attracted to PJI duty.

Bill Forde nominally began his PJI service at Ringway but was transferred almost immediately to Upper Heyford.

After a long stint on Liberators ... I repatriated to UK at cessation of hostilities and became just another flightless bird ... there appeared to be millions of us, painting this, moving that ... An AMO [Air Ministry Order] of the day suggested that Parachute Jumping Instructors were needed and the qualification of PTI/PFO [Physical Training Instructor/Physical Fitness Officer] was required ...

With a strong schoolboy international sporting record plus a couple of aircrew tours Bill felt he was suitably qualified and eventually arrived at Ringway:

... only to be told to take down the training equipment as PTS was moving to Upper Heyford. Took us all afternoon – spoiled the whole day ...

Ron Smith, having served as a PJI in India, returned to PTS at Upper Heyford:

It was bitterly cold and snowing heavily. I was directed to the PTS barrack block ... on entering I was confronted by an Indian bearer ...taking my kit he led me upstairs to a large barrack room and put my kit down by a bed that had already been made up ... I thought I was dreaming. The bearer told me that all the PTS sahibs were having a party and I was expected to join them ... I was greeted by several old pals. I kept asking them about the Indian bearer, but could not get any sort of

answer from any of them ... I never saw the bearer again and
nobody seemed to know anything about him ... was he a ghost
of my imagination or a very cleverly planned joke? ...

Ron has puzzled on that to this day. Upper Heyford had not had
time to acquire too much PJI mythology, so perhaps the bearer
really was a ghost.

So saying, the PTS spirit survived the move easily, and the relief
afforded by peace seemed to allow a more relaxed atmosphere.

Val Valentine (another of the legends during my own PJI
infancy):

A weekend trip to Butlins, Skegness in 1949 for a recruiting
demonstration from the balloon. At midnight after the dance,
a stick of PJIs from the top board into the pool, led by Jimmy
Blyth in No 1 Dress, less jacket [the formal brass-buttoned
tunic] ...

The work, of course, continued apace. British airborne forces,
although somewhat reduced in size, continued to recruit,
thereby producing a steady stream of young trainees.

The course syllabus settled down and eventually had regular
troops attending for up to four weeks to make eight parachute
descents of increasing complexity. Reservists – Territorial Army
(TA) – attended simultaneously but for two weeks to make
seven descents. By the late 1950s and throughout the 60s, 70s
and 1980s this was the basic 'bread and butter' function of the
school.

The process was continuous and newly-qualified PJIs were
allocated to an end-to-end training task. Four weeks with a
regular eight-jump course, followed immediately by another
four-week spell, followed by another. Those working with the

TA would rotate similarly, but at shorter interval. Matters settled at around 60 troops per course: one instructor to every eight trainees or so; a hierarchy of experienced flight sergeants closely supervising it all; a young recently-qualified junior officer held responsible for each course.

An additional and major part of post-war PTS work was formally established during the school's time at Upper Heyford; full-time attachment of RAF PJIs to Army units. Bill Fell was the first to command a detachment with the newly-formed TA airborne units:

In May 1949 I was to be the first PJI attached to the newly-formed 16th Airborne Division (TA) ... HQ in Chelsea ... I received my instructions – namely to coordinate ground training for all the thirty-odd units, and to arrange and assist with the jumping programmes ...

PJI attachment to the Army developed strongly – no doubt reinforced by the existing trust that existed – and by the 1960s there had been a formed-up unit with the regular Airborne at Aldershot for some time. Other PJIs, often alone, served with TA battalions around the country while yet more worked closely with the Royal Marines and other more covert forces.

Stan Roe held an early PTS record for officer PJI service with Airborne units. (It may still stand because Roe appears to have escaped 'career ladder' intervention whereby – usually just as the he was becoming competent – an individual was appointed to non-PJI general duties.) After PTS Stan served at seven 'Army' detachments, and also as a PJI survival instructor:

... [at PTS] in August 1953 ... the parachute training programme board outside the CO's office boasted a 'book' made by McCumiskey [a PJI contemporary of Stan] on the next

officer movements to [the detachment at] 16 Parachute Brigade ... (such posting speculation was a favourite, and sometimes alarming, pastime at PTS).

Stan continued:

The favourite was yours truly. Why me? (Most of us asked this repeatedly during our service.) ... Could it have been that I had just bought a house in Oxford? ... After the usual preamble the CO said he wanted two volunteers and 'Who's going with Stan Roe?' ... this move turned out to be the best in my career, leading to 24 years of continuous service to the Paras ...

Fifteen years later I volunteered for detached service with 16 Parachute Brigade. As it had for Stan, so it proved a good move for me; offering undreamed of opportunity for independent PJI action. So saying, when moved on by the 'career ladder', it proved impossible to describe to my new RAF masters exactly what I had been up to for the previous year or two, and who had paid my wages meanwhile.

The Parachute School's time at Upper Heyford now seems to have been an interlude while more permanent accommodation was found and perhaps the unit's departure was hastened by the decision to turn Heyford into a United States Air Force bomber base. In June 1950 PTS moved to RAF Abingdon taking the complete and unvarying training task with it, together with the more remote-controlled but increasing detachment work with army units.

The drop zone continued at Weston-on-the-Green, it had been close to Upper Heyford, but now required a 20-mile road journey to return the troops to base after their jumps. (In the early days the convoy passed through Oxford city centre thus giving rise to many crewroom tales of troops and PJIs getting up to mischief in the streets.)

It seems that the aircraft also passed over the city on their way to Weston and there is much PTS mythology of parachutists being despatched over the suburbs following some on-board signal confusion or other. Contained in the same volume of legend are the many versions of PJIs who fell from the aircraft 'accidentally' just to see if the despatcher parachute would actually work. This must have been an easy 'mistake' to stage because the PTS workhorse of the day, the Hastings, typically arrived for the day's work at PTS with the port door completely removed. As the training progress involved more parachutists per sortie so the starboard door would be removed during the flight by the PJIs – Hastings's doors were not hinged – thereby creating more mythology that described large bits of aircraft being despatched over the Dreaming Spires.

The 1960s generation of PJIs joined a unit that was very much a major part of RAF Abingdon. The flying squadron based there provided dropping aircraft: the gigantic Beverleys of 47 Squadron gave a fine jumping platform. Hastings and Argosy aircraft came as required from elsewhere and then Abingdon-based Andovers joined the fleet. From time to time a parachuting balloon was moored outside the upwind perimeter track.

In mid-1967 the C130 Hercules was appearing at PTS and it was not long before the earlier machines were phased out. The most immediate effect on the PTS training task of this change was that a single aircraft drill and procedure could be taught, and the system quickly dispelled the many crewroom rumours about slipstream blast outside the door, excessive drop speed and uncomfortable seating. Unfortunately the latter passed equally quickly from gossip to hard fact.

At Abingdon a whole hangar was converted into an undercover ground training area, while a nearby grass area was taken up by a 60-foot high hydraulic jumping tower - dominating the skyline – and the notorious 'knacker cracker'. Both of these ground training equipments were designed to simulate parachute jumping as far as was possible and dated from the latter days of Ringway.

The Parachute Regiment had also established a permanent detachment at PTS: a smaller reversal of the PTS detachments. Known as the Parachute Courses Administration Unit (PCAU) they dealt with all the Army administration of the troops attending the school. Dealing with the RAF administrators on site, and for all ranks, they saw to accommodation, pay, messing and discipline, thereby relieving PTS of that task.

In strict protocol terms, this small regimental team passed the troops to the tender mercies of the PJIs every day, and a morning muster parade outside PTS had been continued from Ringway days for this purpose. It was simple: the school could count trainee heads each day; the senior PJIs could assess the fitness of them to continue and the School Warrant Officer could issue stern daily orders to everybody. It was PCAU that notified the award of the military parachutist qualification – 'wings' – to Army records, but the actual badge was usually presented at a simple PTS-mounted parade.

Arguably, the number of serious incidents at PTS – fatal accidents and life-threatening injuries – during its time at Abingdon was no worse than at Heyford or Ringway. Nonetheless, one record shows eight fatal accidents to trainees between February 1951 and March 1968; half of these deaths were caused by hitting the head on landing. Of course, during that period considerable numbers of parachute training descents occurred, and despite a steady stream of fractures and strains, military parachuting had developed into a remarkably safe activity.

It was tragically ironic, therefore, that the greatest loss of life occurred when an aircraft on its way from Abingdon to drop parachutists at Weston-on-the-Green crashed at Little Baldon, just east of Oxford. There were no survivors: all 41 souls on board perished, including a complete crew of despatcher and parachuting PJIs. The aircraft, a Hastings from 36 Squadron RAF Colerne, had spent the day at PTS mounting several sorties to the drop zone (normal procedure when the weather was favourable) and the fatal flight was to have been the last that day, 6th July 1965.

After the crash the entire Hastings fleet was grounded almost immediately, but returned to service before the year's end. Trainee PJIs jumping from that aircraft in early June 1966 therefore had more than just parachuting fears to overcome: they found themselves in a not-too-well-trusted machine, but worse were the black-humour assurances of the staff PJIs who, in the time-honoured military fashion had had no choice but to carry on regardless.

Nonetheless, the catastrophe was listed as the third-worst UK air crash at that time and is commemorated to this day with a plaque and laid-up flags in the nearby Toot Baldon church. Each anniversary sees a parade of PJIs and Canopy Club members (former PJIs) together with representatives from the Parachute Regiment Association and the flying squadron.

The PTS training task barely faltered, of course but, in the curious way of these events, the ensuing trouble-free period was then broken by three years in which several PJIs lost their lives on duty.

In 1970 Les Hicks was killed making a trial descent with a parachute assembly under development.

The following year saw Ralph Ramshaw and Royston Bullen go into the sea under their parachutes just off a Cyprus beach; Royston swam to safety, but Ralph drowned. Later that year – 9th November – an RAF Hercules flew into the sea off Pisa. All 52 on board were killed, including 46 Italian airborne troops – an awful reprise of the Hastings crash – but worst for PTS was the loss of Ralph Lee the only PJI on board.

The bad run continued into 1972 when on 8th April an Andover carrying the Falcons Parachute Display Team crashed on take-off in Northern Italy. Most survived, but of the four fatalities two were PJIs from the school: Bill Last and Royston Bullen.

I was 'duty dog' at Abingdon that weekend and was instructed to go to Royston's off-base home with the news that he was missing (the deaths had not been confirmed at that stage). As my wife and I, together with a doctor, faced Royston's impossibly young wife, the memory that he had swum to safety only a year earlier almost prevented coherent speech.

Many years later Henry MacDonald remembered that day:

... just another PTS training detachment, in Italy 14 March — 9 April 1972 . . On Saturday 8 April 1972, the day before we were due to return to RAF Abingdon, the Falcons gave a display for all of the personnel at Ampugnano... After the formalities we made our way back to the Andover aircraft prior to departing for Pisa

Whilst taxiing, the ALM informed us that the aircraft would be making a tactical take-off. Very soon after take-off I heard the ALM call out, 'We have lost an – .' It was then that I and many more on board knew that we were going to crash. I got myself further into the seat crash net and just waited for the outcome ...

After the aircraft came to a halt, I made my way to the rear to exit through the ramp which had opened on impact. Several [others] had got out through this gap when suddenly the MS 26, multi seat dingy inflated stopping any other personnel escaping from the back.

... the aircraft was well ablaze and I followed Bob Souter to escape through the cockpit area ... but I was driven back by the fierceness of the flames ... I think it was Dave Ross who located the port side escape exit ... then the remainder of us managed to escape, like rats up a drainpipe ... The reality then set in, we had survived an air-crash but sadly, we had lost friends and colleagues.

Henry went on to describe how, as with all military units, the task continued regardless:

Exactly 10 days later we made our first four training descents at RAF Weston on the Green. This was followed on 29 April by the opening displays of the 1972 RAF Falcons season at RAF Shawbury and Speke Airport ...

Indeed the training task continued relentlessly, but with fewer serious accidents. Nonetheless, the record of that period reminds us that in September 1974 a stick of parachutists fell into the Kiel Canal during a night exercise and six drowned. Although not directly mounted by PTS, the exercise tragedy involved PJIs, airborne and on the ground.

In April 1976 PTS deployed from Abingdon to RAF Brize Norton in West Oxfordshire. Training was partially restricted or staged at Aldershot – no question of cancellation – during the physical move, but to me, returning that week after a tour away, it certainly seemed unpopular amongst the PJIs. Many had strong domestic ties to Abingdon and although Brize Norton was not so far away, it seemed to be step too far. Also it was if PTS had given up being a long-term biggish fish in a little pond and was now a small, specialised unit of doubtful provenance cast into a conventional, and very big, lake.

Matters were not improved by our arriving at a time when the RAF's world-girdling transport fleet was being severely cut – two long-range aircraft types being withdrawn – resulting in squads of morose aircrew being given odd jobs to do. Into all this PTS arrived accompanied by squads of soldiers, Marines and other 'brown jobs'. We also attracted a 'smelly old Hercules' at regular intervals – not polished 'shiny fleet' operations at all – and then compromised our reluctant welcome by asking almost at once if we could drop free-fall parachutists onto the airfield.

Many of my duties during this 'settling-in' period required me to liaise with the base administrative and other support staffs. PTS was frequently described as 'oddball' during this period; there were other, less kindly suggestions too.

And the Parachute School has been at RAF Brize Norton to this day.

4.   A REFINEMENT OR TWO

The mid-1960s generation of PJIs entered a ground training environment that was little changed from that shown in the antique films we studied. These illustrated perfect parachute landing rolls performed by solemn instructors who began each demonstration on thick coir mats from a stiff position of erect military attention and ended equally so. Puffs of dust accompanied the action and the more professional wore their beret throughout; collars and ties were, of course, de rigueur. Around the training area suspended parachute harnesses vied for space with ladder-like platforms that gradually accustomed trainees to make landing rolls at speed.

Parachute-dropping aircraft had become 'user-friendly'. The procedure whereby a small group of parachutists shuffled in turn on their backsides towards the edge of a hole in the floor had been superseded before the end of the war by more than twice the number of men lining up and proceeding upright through a door. By the mid-1950s aircraft with a parachuting door on each side had become common, thus carrying more troops and allowing them to jump simultaneously to land in the target area with less scatter.

The balloon continued very much in evidence. It too was almost unchanged and in world-wide parachute training systems almost unique to the British Military. (One exception was Belgium where a bigger balloon and cage had been developed together with a way of keeping the balloon inflated and under cover between training programmes.)

In a busy, seemingly endless training regime, with no room for passengers, there continued to be an overpowering need for newcomers to learn quickly: especially as many of the pioneers were still serving.

In the mid-1950s a very visible change to British military parachuting was the introduction of the reserve parachute. Supposedly to meet a NATO requirement – the Americans had carried one through their airborne history – the reserve, however, was not universally welcomed. Peter Hearn recorded this reluctance – it had never been in military use for several tens of thousands of descents, so why start now?

... there were those who considered it to be a damn nuisance ...
For the soldier, it was extra weight: it was less ammunition.
For the PJI it grossly obstructed his view of the ground coming up to meet his boots for those immaculate stand-up landings...

As one who had never jumped without the comfort of a reserve parachute, Hearn readily conceded his admiration for those generations who had done so as a matter of course. He told a nice story of an Italian parachutist who jumped with a reserve for the first time in his career and had to use it too. Far from being grateful for the life-saving loan, he was heard to complain bitterly:

The first time I wear a second 'chute what happens? My
bloody main [parachute] does not openı ...

Nonetheless, all British military parachutists began to carry a reserve parachute clipped separately onto the front of the harness. It remains there to this day for static line parachutes and only the introduction of the advanced ram-air parachute to PTS in the late 1970s saw the reserve incorporated into the backpack. Even then it was to be another couple of years or so before the reserve's canopy performance matched that of the main or primary.

All PTS trainees were drilled in, and practiced during ground training, a one-stop immediate reaction to any doubt about their main parachute: 'Pull Your Reserve'. Experienced PJIs knew that if a pulled reserve inflated at once during an emergency then it had been needed. However, 'interesting moments' could arise if a reserve was pulled accidentally in the trainee's excitement or too hastily when the main canopy was still developing to full support. The reserve – at that stage a bundle of formless nylon – could tangle with the main, collapse it and then fail to inflate itself.

My own painful memory of this is centred on a coroner's court where, as a newly-qualified PJI, I found it impossible to explain why I had instructed the trainee to pull his reserve under what became a self-correcting minor malfunction of his main. As a layman, the Coroner naturally asked the simple question, *'Could it be said that pulling the reserve resulted in the man's death?'* Followed by, *'If that is so, why did you so instruct?'*

Not many instructors cared to debate the definition of 'too hasty' a reserve pulling, but as there could be no time for academic debate while under stress in the air, an immediate reaction had to be drilled. Nonetheless, in the mid-1960s we were all glad when the school abandoned the practice of deploying a reserve during a demonstration descent under a perfect main.

So, the chest-mounted reserve certainly became a life-saver but it did pose the occasional training and operating dilemma. The risk was always greater if, following a mid-air entanglement between parachutists, a reserve was then deployed into the mix-up above. PTS training always suggested a clear-headed cautious assessment here – knowledge dispels fear – not always possible in the heat of the moment.

A development of the reflex 'Pull Your Reserve' training (that might worsen an already hesitant canopy development) became necessary by the early 1980s. Advanced freefall parachutes were common at PTS so requiring training in the practice of discarding, or 'cutting away', a malfunctioned main canopy, falling free and then operating the reserve into 'clean' air. Even then the results could include a large slice of luck as Dave Armstrong recalled:

I had collided with another parachutist [both under their main parachutes] ... entirely my fault ... we started to rotate and lose height rapidly ... at approximately 1000 feet I had only one option and cutaway ...

Under his small reserve parachute Dave made a safe landing in a car park and looked up at the other parachutist still rotating violently but with Dave's discarded main wrapped around him:

He couldn't cutaway because of my parachute so in desperation he pulled his reserve which luckily went behind and above his square [the rotating main canopy]. It inflated perfectly and stopped him rotating. He looked quite spectacular with three parachutes ... but thankfully managed to land without injury ...

These men were highly experienced advanced PJIs, and it would have been difficult to write a training schedule for such possibilities. Even so, Dave noted:

So what did I learn? ... 'never switch off' ... parachuting is equally dangerous in training, exercise or real situations ... It [the incident] gave me tremendous confidence in the PTS training ... remain calm, follow what you have been taught, you have a good chance of surviving ...

None of the 'Old, Old Boys' who awed us in the mid-1960s would have jumped without a reserve by then, but they never missed a chance to tell us that we beginners 'had it soft'. Such scorn was, of course, in the full tradition of putting newcomers in their proper place, but in hindsight it does reinforce the fact that basic principles had not changed markedly and that Louis Strange, Maurice Newnham, JCK, *et al* had established robust and effective ground rules from the very beginning.

In the same way that post-war and present-day PJIs rarely acknowledge openly the potential dangers of their work, so it was with the 'Ringway' men. However, their excitement at being part of a revolutionary military ethos, and devising ways to better the training for this, comes over strongly in their written memories:

Johnny Dawes, one of the original Army instructors at Ringway and loaned to the RAF during the change-over period, described his first jump:

With a great effort of will I dared to look down [from the balloon] on my first bird's eye view of the English countryside. To my horror I saw five hundred feet below a tiny stretcher with a dark motionless figure being lifted into a blood-wagon...

One of the great advantages for PTS of using the balloon was that the novice parachutist's descent passage was predictable thus allowing instruction through a loudhailer from the ground. Clearly this had been recognised from the beginning and continued throughout the balloon's use at PTS until the early 1990s.

Such was not so straightforward for trainee descents from aircraft. A variety of wheeled, battery-powered loudhailer systems were tried over the years (one version could pick up

Radio Oxford by holding the microphone aloft), but the basic problem remained: the exact position in the sky of each trainee could not be predicted. Consequently, and despite the avowed fitness of the instructors, a sometimes lengthy sprint followed by breathless disjointed word of wisdom was never going to be the solution. My generation frequently doubted whether the troops ever heard us anyway, let alone react. Perhaps it was just as well that one of Louis Strange's ideas came to nothing:

I had tried to get horses for the instructors to ride up and down the line of paratroops giving instructions to them with megaphones ...

What had definitely not changed was the alarm the newly qualified PJI felt when having to pass on the knowledge to the trainees for the first time. Things were easier for us, of course; we were entering a discipline that had a 20-year plus pedigree: the whole business of parachuting was less 'suck-it-and-see'. That did not lessen the beginners' fright, but at least as instructors we could assume a jaunty posture to the trainees:

"It'll be OK, son, easy as falling off a log."

Needless to say, the older PJIs would invoke their own mantra – especially to new PJI officers:

"It's all mind over matter. We don't mind and you don't matter."

Peter Hearn recalled being required to march with the troops (the norm at PTS) and put at ease by his instructor:

"No class distinction 'ere. Officers 'it the ground as 'ard as 'umans!"

At Ringway in 1941 things were a bit more experimental: equipment was under development; a way of landing without injury, and the teaching of that, was embryonic; meanwhile the number of trainees was increasing – PTS had to get on with things.

Erroll Minter, a decorated and much respected 'father-figure' at PTS in the mid-1960s recalled:

I went on parade on 1st November 1941 with just two balloon descents under my belt – to teach the Army how to become parachutists ...

Erroll also quickly learned from the School Warrant Officer how to cover for lack of knowledge:

If you get stuck in your synthetic [ground] training or if someone asks you a question you can't answer ... double march them three times round the hangar ...

It wasn't long before various academics and other agencies took an interest in the new style of warfare. The whole dread business of parachuting seems to have been an awesome fascination for all manner of people throughout PTS history. (Even when sport parachuting had become commonplace by the 1970s and descending canopies were no longer the traffic-stoppers they had been, the school continued to attract visitors seemingly mesmerised by the prospect of jumping out of a perfectly serviceable aircraft.)

Harry Ward, a pre-war professional 'stunt' parachutist, recorded a Ringway incident that persisted as a PTS legend throughout my time. A researcher was keen to examine the effect of a refusal to parachute on other, willing, troops. He was allowed to go up in the balloon, complete with parachute, to see for himself:

... the boffin was keen to examine the effects of a 'refusal' on the rest of the troops ... So at six hundred feet ... our little head-shrinker braced himself at the aperture and cried loudly, 'I refuse to jump! I refuse to jump!'

'Like bloody 'ell you do!' muttered the despatcher, and hurled the protesting figure bodily out ...

No doubt the PJIs at Ringway quickly came to terms with trainees who refused to parachute, as did their post-war successors. By the mid-1960s a long-established procedure saw to a quick removal of the 'refusal' from PTS followed by his return to unit. Partly-sympathetic interviews by a PJI officer and/or a doctor could be included in this, but it was the PJI on the spot who took the immediate action.

A refusal in the balloon cage tended to be less tricky than in an aircraft: there were fewer trainees for the PJI to handle and the balloon was not flying along with a line of parachutists aiming to leave the door in short order. In the balloon cage the PJI might give the refusal a second chance after the others had gone, but more likely that would be unsuccessful, or unwise, and a crestfallen descent would ensue.

In the back of an aircraft a refusal, especially in a moving line or 'stick' could lead to two or more men – possibly attempting to close a gap – trying to pass through the door together; always a bad move when jumping with static line parachutes.

The usual progress for regular troops was that their first jump would follow five days of intensive ground training and preparation; slightly less for Territorials.

Doubtless the press of war resulted in a shorter course and preparation time at Ringway, but, even so, one newly-recruited PJI made his first jump in what is probably still a PTS record time. Harry Ward recalled:

When he reported in his best uniform to Louis Strange ... the boss sent him straight to me for training. 'You're in luck,' I said. 'We've got a kite going off for a dropping sortie in a few minutes.' I had him fitted with an 'X' type [the standard military parachute of the day] ... A few minutes later, over Tatton Park [the training drop zone] and still wearing his best uniform, he jumped ahead of seven Norwegian troops. He had been at Ringway almost an hour. Nothing like the 'deep end' method I always thought ...

PTS had long been required to train for parachuting into the sea as a military option. My generation of PJIs were regaled on arrival at the school with incredible stories – and film – of parachutists leaving the aircraft: one carrying an inflatable boat in its valise; the next man a hefty outboard engine; the third fuel and so on. To our wide-eyed awe it looked as if the load was carried by the parachute with the man fastened on as an afterthought; normal movement appeared impossible. Meanwhile, our seniors would solemnly assure us that the despatchers' job on these occasions was to lift each man in turn off the floor, hold him in the slipstream and let go.

When it came to our turn to try jumping into the sea for the first time (without the boat) matters were not improved by learning that the approved technique on approaching the water – a hundred feet up or so – was to unlock the harness and partially un-strap oneself. Having passed our parachuting career to that point refusing to contemplate any such action until firmly on the ground, such a briefing seemed to contradict everything we had been taught. Needless to say, we would then be regaled with matter-of-fact tales of troops letting go of the harness too high. It was all mind over matter: *we don't mind and you don't matter.*

Perhaps Maurice Newnham foresaw such antics when he introduced a uniquely PTS Christmas celebration that, curiously, did not catch on and happily did not survive until my time:

At ten o'clock on the morning of Christmas Day half a dozen of us performed the Ringway Ceremony, which I had inaugurated the year before, known as 'The Mortification of the Flesh. The ritual was quite simple – we parachuted from 700ft into the deep waters of Rostherne Mere. This was regarded by a very few as a suitable prelude to the day's festivities. I noticed, however, that of the previous year's enthusiasts only one, Joe Sunderland, felt the necessity for being mortified with me a second time. As the temperature was 40 degrees Fahrenheit and the wind stung like a whip, the decision was perhaps not altogether surprising ...

Would the Ringway PJIs, and those of the 1950s and 1960s scorn later techniques: wet and dry suits, the boat already inflated on a pallet with its own parachute and, much later, steerable parachutes allowing close grouping in the sea?

5.   THE EXCITEMENT, PERHAPS EVEN FEAR

The PTS badge was approved by King George VI in July 1944. It shows an open parachute carrying the torch of knowledge all enclosed in the standard RAF heraldic frame surmounted by the crown, all atop the words: *Knowledge Dispels Fear*. As in most heraldry this motto is proudly direct in its message, and neatly summarises the PTS objectives.

Who exactly composed the words appears not to be known but it is likely that, like many who followed, he experienced the occasional reversal of them. It has been said by many a military parachutist, and that includes PJIs, that the man who claims never to have been afraid is lying, or has a very poor memory.

If an extended definition of *fear* embraces anxiety, apprehension, or excitement caused by the presence or anticipation of danger, then there was always plenty of that at PTS; particularly excitement.

Fear is a simple word, an emotion uncomplicated by modern euphemisms of 'adrenalin rush', 'heightening of the senses' or 'flight or fight'. There is no shame in its experience for a healthy adult and PTS mythology frequently recalls many fearful moments for instructors and trainees alike. Even during 'routine' jumps – some might say, *especially during* – by very experienced parachutists unexpected predicaments could occur without warning.

Sometimes beginners' 'moments' might stretch into agonising hours – days – of anticipation: that very first jump; the first night descent (especially from the silent balloon). For PJIs: the first freefall; the first jump after a period away from PTS; a display jump in marginal winds into a tight drop zone. The list could be endless and was always, of course, varied by the individual's state-of-mind on the day.

Naturally, PJIs would never confess to any of this, but the unit frequently enjoyed a lively buzz of apprehension, anticipation and excitement.

'Okay,' PJIs might say to trainees. 'Maybe jumping out of fully serviceable aeroplanes is not too normal, but if you do what we say, you'll be okay.' A robust matter-of-fact acceptance of the risks became the PTS creed from Day One of each training course. Outsiders occasionally likened the preparatory ground training to 'brain-washing': producing drilled automatons that just jumped out simply because that was next in the sequence.

I never met a robotic PJI – far from it – nor in truth not too many trainee parachutists either; though without doubt, 'peer-pressure' might compel the more fearful to follow the herd.

Ask most military parachutists if they remember the instructor who first 'threw them out' (needless to say 'throwing' was strictly forbidden, but 'gentle persuasion' of the reluctant was common). All will remember all too clearly: they may not recall the name, but the occasion is seared into the sub-conscious. (Well into my own retirement my young niece's partner, a former Royal Marine, told me in vivid detail of his own first-jump twenty five years earlier.)

Of course, being a British unit there was a strong ethos of 'stiff-upper-lip'. Perhaps that is what produced the apparent calm amongst the trainees. However, one only had to witness the explosive relief, joy and near-religious fervour that appeared in the first seconds after a successful first parachute jump to know that PTS was probably getting things right. There could be a deal of 'kissing' the wonderfully solid grass on those occasions and, had it not been a manly fashion in those days, there might have been some PJI-hugging too.

Les Males vividly recalled his 'moment' in 1946:

The interior of the Dakota is dim and the glare from the green fields and the surrounding sky from the open door reflects on the silhouettes of the men in front. The dispatcher stands in the door and sticks his head outside – the slipstream flaps his hair and his cheek quiver like jelly. The floor sways, trembles a little and the engines roar suddenly softens a little which means the Dakota is slowing down to the exit speed of 90 knots ...

The slipstream thunders ... Everyone is infectiously cheerful. And prompted by the atmosphere, suggestions referring to possible dangers are hilariously shouted and applauded... You acknowledge there is a slight risk in jumping and you say to yourself, "Please God, help me!"

The first jumper exits ... and within a second we are all running for the door ... then every second is analysed: clearly and distinctly. You are suspended outside the doorway in the cold harsh slipstream of the thundering engines. "Space, space, and freedom." Those in front of you are like toy soldiers swinging on strings of unopened parachutes, silhouetted against a colourful landscape.

Looking backwards over your head you can see the periphery of the 'chute which is like a pair of puckered lips hesitating to open. Wild possibilities crowd your excited brain until with a soft sarcastic "pop" the canopy billows out and all is peaceful ... it seems fantastic as though you were living a dream. The earth is moving slowly beneath your feet ... but with the descent begins to move faster and faster ... The grass rushing underfoot becomes a green blur and the prospect of the shattering impact is felt – with some reluctance. It's going to be a heavy landing.

Oh, Christ! Everything slams into you. Earth like iron thumps every part of your body ... With an effort, the parachute is collapsed and you are free to stand up in a wide sunny field to look around and wonder ... What an interesting world it is, and how wonderful it is to live in it!

In the canteen afterwards, young men in grassed-stained jackets streaked with earth are talking "shop" ... of exits, twists and thrown-lines, oscillations, ground winds and other problems of parachuting. The Transport NCO calls out over the hubbub ... you remember the prayer you made not long ago. Very sincerely you say "Thank you, God!"

I certainly remember mine: both 'moment' and PJI. It was March 1965 and in the care of Wilf Jones my death seemed imminent as the trainee group before me went aloft in the balloon cage.

Four of us gazed upwards with unseeing eyes as first one, two and three opening parachutes were followed by a long, long pause.

The balloon began its descent. The fourth first-jumper was coming down with it. He had become a non-jumper, a refusal: poised on the very edge he could not do it. It was wonderful encouragement for we who followed. Did we jump to prove a point? Had we too little imagination? No, we jumped out of fear; fear of what Wilf might actually do to follow his threat.

'There'll be none of that nonsense when you're up there.'

And there wasn't, but what really frightened us was the 'rocket' delivered by the PTS Commanding Officer, a Ringway man. Jumpers or not, our group had offended the credo.

Many Years later Wilf also remembered that morning, (perhaps because most of the successful jumpers became PJIs eventually). As well as the telling-off he recorded that:

We suffered brown skid-marks in our pants...

Much of the PTS introduction to parachuting was based upon a series of assumptions: we're great instructors; the kit is reliable; we do this every day. These and many others were implanted in the newly-arrived trainee's mind from the start. Only after a day or two did we admit to the possibility of problems: If the parachute doesn't open, you've always got another one; look out for mid-air collisions.

Black humour often sugared the pill; a mind-set that dates from the very beginnings:

'Say, Sarge', asked one innocent in the days before reserve parachutes were carried. 'Suppose I jump out and the 'chute doesn't open? What then?'

'I'd say you were jumping to a conclusion.'...

Another 'Ringway' PJI, Peter Tingle wrote:

When he jumped from the aircraft, his 'chute didn't open ... Roman Candle ... He hit the ground and bounced and the parachute descended over him like a shroud... We didn't bother to run because we knew he would be dead.

However, the parachute suddenly moved ... and this white-faced, six-foot Liverpudlian sat up and said, 'I didn't do a very good landing, did I, Sarge?

'Lie down, Scouse. You should be dead,' we told him.

Dick Mullins, who trained as a PJI immediately after the war, and was to command PTS in the late 1960s, recalled how the PTS system was designed to put newcomers at ease:

The senior instructor gave us our initial talk and this was followed by the showing of a film about Clem Sohn [a pre-war birdman] jumping to his death. The sequence showed Clem in difficulty ... fortunately for those watching the film the sight of the impact was obscured by the spectators at the show ...

Fear, anticipation, excitement, whatever we choose to call it, can have different effects according to mood and circumstances, but it was always worse at the beginning.

Peter Hearn recalled his 'excitement' vividly. First-ever jump; from the balloon:

All the moisture had drained from my throat and seeped into my knees. The Flight Sergeant had stopped talking. The silence was terrifying ... Perhaps they had lost the signal flag. Perhaps we'd have to go down. Perhaps ... He stepped back suddenly and the metal bar dropped with a clatter like the clap of doom ... No more chat. No more Bob's your uncle. Just a statement of fact that propelled me against all reason into the open, swaying door to stand trembling on the edge of eight hundred feet of nothing ...

Peter became one of the pioneers of PTS freefall and display parachuting. Without doubt he would enjoy many more excit-

ing/fearful moments, but arguably none as alarming as the first
– it happened to all of us.

Geoff Greenland, the 1968 display team leader, had an exciting
landing at Biggin Hill:

*It was a misty, squally sort of day. We could only manage a
hop and pop from 3000ft. I just managed to land on the edge
of the DZ. It was really gusty, and before I could get the
canopy down, I was off across the pans, being dragged on my
backside. The next thing I knew was a sudden battering as the
canopy and myself were whip-lashed under the fuselage of an
aircraft. When I got out, my helmet was fractured ... and the
canopy in shreds wrapped round the props of a Mustang.
Another couple of turns and I'd have been in there too. All I
got was a busted finger, a bang on the nose and a rollicking
from Val when she read it in the papers next day.*

Although the PJIs quickly became adept at spotting potential
problem trainees, predicting refusals was next-to-impossible:
so, take every one as he appears was as good a rule as any. It did
happen occasionally that a trainee would be removed from the
course for other-than-outright-refusal reasons: repeated
hesitation at the aircraft door; not displaying a positive deter-
mination; lack of alertness. This latter was rare: the heightened
awareness caused by fear ensured that all trainees listened
carefully and performed promptly, whatever their intellect.

Even so, many non-PJI parachutists never entirely overcame
their fear – probably because they rarely did as much jumping
as PJIs – and occasionally there was hesitation amongst the
qualified.

Grahame May recalled one typical 'moment':

During the early 1970s when members of the Parachute Regiment had to complete four descents a year to qualify for Para Pay, it was not unusual for parachute programmes to be generated at short notice to facilitate this rule.

On one such occasion, a balloon programme, the normal motley crew of jumpers of mature experience and rank paraded to go through the motions of pure hell and torture ... two-way radios were used between the ground and despatcher and on one particular cage the last man to jump was an old soldier who had seen action during the Suez Crisis ... when I called him to the door he promptly broke out in a sweat, had a glazed look on his face and was gasping for breath.

When I finally manoeuvred him into the door and levered both his hands away from the uprights [frame], I afforded him due respect by whispering "Go when you are ready." Five minutes later I asked, "Are you going?" to which he replied "I'm not ready".

This situation naturally called for subtle action so, pretending to push the transmit button on the radio, I calmly said, "One refusal – close haul." The old boy's response was his version of a forceful exit but in fact was a snivelling stumble out of the door, during which he hit his parachute pack on the sill, performing an immaculate forward somersault through his rigging lines.

Grahame, of course, was fully aware that a refusal to jump by a trained, badge-wearing military parachutist would result in court-martial. Such incidents were rare but not unknown and PJIs became trusted mentors in the back of the aircraft or in a dark, trembling balloon cage.

The 'official' golden rule applied to all trainees (at least post-war) was that a trainee who refused would never be given another chance. For sure, a PJI despatching from a balloon cage might well employ all manner of subterfuge in the face of hesitation. Once that cage, or aircraft, was back on the ground, however, the refusal's military parachuting career was over: at PTS a swift return to the home unit usually followed. It was not unknown for young refusals, latest in a family pedigree of Airborne service, to plead for, 'Just another go, I wasn't ready first time.' Almost without exception, the PJI would know that the man was as ready as he was ever going to be, and that instant judgement would carry the day.

An Army padre began his hesitations – hindsight being all-seeing – as soon as he left the ground level for higher bits of ground training equipment. Eventually, he 'stuck' in the balloon cage; he simply could not take that step forward. During his post-refusal interview he pleaded unsuccessfully for a second attempt. Who he contacted after that was unknown, but PTS was asked 'semi-officially' via a sort of ecclesiastical old-boys' net to give their man a second chance – after a period of 'meditation.' This was reluctantly agreed; the padre underwent another dose of preparatory ground training and stuck on the edge again.

Fatal accidents, serious injury and refusals during basic training could infect course morale and mood at a time when the word *survival* could best describe the ambition of some that remained. The PJIs' task, of course, was to progress the training relentlessly. There was little time for searching analysis of fears and doubts. The great majority had no need for that anyway.

Peter McCumiskey was training Territorial Army soldiers and catches the atmosphere nicely:

It was the early 1950s and Teddy Boys were very much in fashion: typical Teddy Boy haircut; jumping jacket nipped in at the waist and padded in the shoulders; beret at a jaunty angle. The only things missing were the "winkle pickers". He affected a mincing gait which made him look slightly effeminate.

He had just made his third aircraft descent on a glorious summer evening and was rolling up his chute with the re-mainder of his course, when the Hastings ran in to drop the final stick. One parachute completely malfunctioned and the unfortunate trainee plummeted to the ground. It was before reserve chutes were introduced and he didn't have a chance. The excited chatter and banter, usual between trainees who had just completed an aircraft descent, stopped abruptly giving way to a shocked and eerie silence.

The following morning when the course paraded, a significant number had their suitcases packed ready to go home. In the Teddy Boy's section of ten, he was the only one to continue – the other nine went home.

He completed the course and on the "wings parade". I con-gratulated him for carrying on when all his mates had packed in.

His reply, "Well I've got my effing self-respect to think of."

The trust that developed between trainees and PJIs was consid-erable and it continued into qualified parachutist service. For all their scorn of the 'Brylcream Boys', the 'Raff Crabs', the average, tough airborne soldier preparing for a parachute sortie – opera-tional or training – was invariably glad to see badge-wearing PJIs embarked as aircraft despatcher crew.

A famous PTS legend about trust persisted throughout my time. It had its beginnings in Maurice Newnham's Ringway days:

A company of Gurkhas were told that they had been chosen to fly over the enemy and jump down on them from 600ft. A little later three rather nervous Gurkhas asked to see their Company Commander. The spokesman explained that they had been thinking about the jumping from aeroplanes and weren't at all sure that they could do it. The height of 600ft seemed too high; could the aircraft to come down to 200ft? But, they were told, it's much safer from 600ft because it gives the parachute more time to open.

Oh, we didn't know we were to have parachutes, said the deputation. That makes it quite all right ...

There developed, of course, as many ways of coping with the fear, the excitement, the stimulation as there were different fears, excitements and stimulations.

Peter Hearn recalled an early freefall jump: already an experienced static line parachutist, he found himself fumbling for familiar bits of equipment:

I stood up, and looked for my strop, and felt silly and a bit sick because there wasn't one. No hooking up this time. I felt naked without a static line ...

Everything went well; his parachute really worked. He asked himself, what had he been so frightened about?

Whatever it was, I was still frightened by it the second, the third and for many more times to come ... fear in the waiting and the anticipation and the early mornings; [and the middle-

of-the-nights] exhilaration in action; and a satisfying sense of
achievement in retrospect ...

For the office-bound PJI, however the elation surrounding a
parachute descent could bring blessed relief:

I had given him [the leading parachutist] two or three seconds
before stepping out over the familiar landscape ... allowing the
canopy to lower me gently down – it was a lovely afternoon.
No 'IN' tray full of paperwork ... what a truly delightful way to
earn a living ...

In the late 1980s as one of a parachute despatch crew in a
Hercules aircraft I was preparing the troops for their jump after
a long low-level bumpy night flight. The senior parachutist on
board was the Brigade Commander. I knew he had not jumped
for some while. He knew that I knew but could not, as he yelled
in my ear, have been more pleased to see a PJI that he recognised. Every trooper in that aircraft got the same careful
attention: we were simply following the code of our predeces-
sors.

6. JUMPING BEANS

Most RAF pilots of my acquaintance were convinced that parachutists, particularly PJIs, were certifiable. To jump out of a perfectly serviceable aircraft was madness: to instruct others in that insanity beggared credibility. Still, they would say in wonderment, what else can you expect from 'Jockstrappers' of the Physical Fitness persuasion?

Almost simultaneous with the agreement that the Parachute Training School (PTS), newly renamed from Central Landing Establishment, should be an RAF unit was it allowed that the instructors, the PJIs, should be found from the Physical Fitness Branch of that service. The branch has changed names several times since 1941, but the essential staffing policy for PTS remains: Physical Education officers (PEdOs) and Physical Training Instructor NCOs (PTIs) only are eligible to qualify as PJIs.

Despite occasional efforts to make up PJI manning shortfall by posting reluctant PTIs into the school for what was little better than ill-disguised 'persuasion by association', PJIs were always found from volunteers. Part of physical education duties on flying stations included parachute ground training for aircrew so every new PEdO and PTI was required to attend an elementary course at PTS that normally included four parachute descents. On completion each man was usually asked: *subject to selection would you be willing to train as a PJI?*

In 1965 I welcomed the question. In the excited flush of five parachute jumps that week the parachute school seemed to offer a fearful, but heroically exciting career; preferable by far to peddling physical fitness to an air force seemingly not too interested.

In the post-war period there was also an occasional attempt to recruit PJIs from other branches. Notably in my memory was in the mid 1970s when word passed around – reinforced, apparently, by a written suggestion from the staffs – that the RAF Regiment could be a fertile breeding ground for Parachute Jumping Instructors. Horror of horrors: 'shop-floor' resistance to this heresy was considerable, even if the Regiment did include a parachute-capable squadron in its organisation.

The irritating irony was that PJIs – particularly noticeable amongst the NCOs – continued to be examined, promoted and paid as ground tradesmen. It was not unknown for a newly-qualified PJI to pass the rest of his RAF career on those duties, yet be required to sit promotion examinations in which the existence of PTS and its work was barely acknowledged. Earlier training in 'gym' work had long been dormant, yet had to be remembered for promotion examinations.

Jake McLoughlin, a decorated and time-served survivor of non-commissioned and commissioned PJI service recalled:

Most PJIs had little time for the PT world. Nevertheless, we were still required to take the same promotion exams as 'ordinary' PTIs. Norman Hoffman came across one difficult question in the Sports and Games paper, which asked, 'What is a fair return in Squash?' Four pence per glass, wrote Norman ...

From the beginning Maurice Newnham had fought for the status of the RAF PJI. He recalled one particular nonsense that probably stemmed from the change-over from joint training responsibility to that of Air Force only:

There had been a moral understanding that they [volunteers for training as parachute instructors] would be given the rank of sergeant with its attendant privileges ... despite the merits of their case these brave and patriotic men found that they were to be fobbed off with sergeants' stripes in unpaid acting rank ... Further, it transpired they were awarded no distinguishing parachute badge and therefore no parachuting pay – both of which privileges were accorded to the Army instructors who, ironically enough, were not supposed to be parachute instructors at all ...

Newnham's account of these and similar unpromising beginnings comes over quite angrily and slow recognition of PJIs by authority appears to have been an irritation for the rest of his time at Ringway.

Eventually, after he and many of the [original] instructors had left the Service, approval was given in late 1945 for an aircrew badge – flying brevet – to be worn by RAF PJIs. Maurice's rueful comment on that belated event makes a poignant end to his record of the fight against indifference:

Oh, well! The war had been won and, although the men who had done most of the work did not receive the recognition they coveted, it would be nice for those who carried on the duties in peacetime. C'est la vie!

The badge is, of course, quite distinctive and could be said to 'mark' PJIs for the rest of their service. Occasionally over the years internal, albeit unofficial, disquiet would arise amongst the ranks of the small branch: non-PJIs would take any opportunity – not always in jest – to be scathing about our desertion of PEd principles.

Advances in parachute equipment and techniques emphasised that PJI work had little in common with that of the PTI in the gymnasium or, more scathingly from the PJI viewpoint, *'in the sports store folding rugby kit'.*

There had been a 'trade' badge during the war, of course, seemingly not remembered with any great affection by those who wore it. Jimmy Young recorded a typical memory of the device:

It was during the period when we didn't have a brevet, just that obnoxious badge of a parachute surrounded by a laurel wreath, sewn on your arm above your stripes. There used to be lots of jibes about this badge like, 'Are you in the RAF badminton team?'

Of course, the new 'half-wing' brevet was properly authorised and promulgated in regulations, but the January 1946 edition of *Tee Emm* takes a rather mischievous slant:

Do You Know What This Is? [Asks the headline above a badly drawn PJI brevet]... . it's a new brevet recently approved by the Air Council for certain new recruits to aircrew status ... It is for RAF Parachute Training Instructors ... largely concerned with 'Red Devil' training ... they have had to fly on ops, been wounded, killed and have been awarded – many of them – decorations for gallantry ... they have frequently been pulled up by Service Police [before the brevet] who want to know why they're wearing an AFC or AFM when they have no aircrew badge. Imposters, hey...

Ron Smith, while serving at No3 PTS, Chaklala in India, recalled preparations to receive the newly-authorised half-wing parachute brevet in December 1945:

The date of the parade was fast approaching but no brevets had arrived from the UK, so arrangements were implemented for a sufficient number to be made by a badge maker in Delhi … proved to be of the highest quality being embroidered with silk thread and padded … An impressive [presentation] parade duly took place … on the following day the question arose as to who was to pay for them? … the instructors were told that they would have to cover the cost … not at all popular … the problem was solved by a benevolent Station Commander footing the bill from his Station Fund … Later the issue brevets arrived from UK and were of such poor quality that those who wanted additional brevets purchased them from the local bazaar . .

As late as 1966 padded brevets could still be seen, and 60 years after that parade Ron still had a handful of those superb badges.

The PJI brevet came with the unusual, possibly unprecedented grant of 'Honorary Aircrew Status', a nebulous definition that persisted throughout my time as a PJI, and does to this day. Such became especially puzzling when, by the mid-1980s, non-PJI rear-crew aircrew – Air Quartermasters, then Air Loadmasters – had long ceased to despatch parachutists. (This undoubtedly came as a relief to the individuals if only because as Loadmaster recruits they no longer were required to make personal parachute jumps themselves.)

So, PJIs were embarked as crew on all sorties where men were to be dropped. Further, in the mid-1980s, they were included in an examination scheme applied to all branches of RAF transport aircrew whereby they had to demonstrate and maintain levels of proficiency in their role. These levels could vary between training and operational function, but as all PJIs were required to be ready for operational flying and despatching, achievement of the highest standard was encouraged.

By the late 1980s the flying regulations and operating procedures for personnel parachute-dropping aircraft specified in some detail the numbers of PJIs to be included in the crew. Those rules also imposed upon PJIs similar flying hours limitations to those applied to 'front-end' crew. Any default could cause abandonment of the sortie.

A major airborne exercise, involving perhaps seven or eight aircraft carrying four PJI crew each, could easily stretch PTS's resources to the point where ab-initio parachute training had to be temporarily curtailed.

Similarly, advanced operational parachuting and training had progressed by the late 1970s to the point where PJIs – usually at NCO rank – could be working in the back of an un-pressurised aircraft at night and at considerable altitude. They would be responsible for the oxygen welfare, preparation and safe parachute despatch of a dozen or more parachutists. Even at low level a PJI team could be handling up to 90 fully armed parachutists per aircraft. Certainly, an aircrew Loadmaster would be in charge 'down the back end' – as would ultimately be the aircraft captain – but, as I came to argue, PJIs under those circumstances were aircrew by any definition.

And yet, as had continued since the war, the PJI NCO was classed, examined and promoted as a ground tradesman.

A specialist rate of additional pay had survived from the Ringway days, but even this had, over the years, been at risk. In the early 1960s there were stories a-plenty of PJIs being denied their specialist pay (and for some, paid acting rank) while returning from the Far East by troop ship: sometimes a two-month period.

Similarly, qualified PJIs posted off parachute duties, but willing to be re-appointed eventually, could only retain the specialist rate of pay by making a minimum of four parachute jumps a year; all properly recorded in a flying log book. To fulfil this requirement men could be attached to PTS for a week during which time they would 'refresh' on personal parachuting skills and equipment. In practice what commonly happened is that the attachment took place during a period of poor weather when the man would quickly 'catch-up' on equipment developments then pass most of the time yarning with old mates while waiting for conditions to improve. As time began to run out he might then join a trainee balloon programme (itself desperately trying to fit into a 'weather window') make four descents in quick succession, learn nothing and run a high risk of injury through lack of practice.

Sometimes fewer than four jumps could be made – or none at all – or the home unit was unable to release the PJI from his appointed duties (it would cost more in lost services than money saved). In such cases it was not unknown for additional pay to be stopped, even 'clawed back'.

Thankfully, this nonsense ceased in early1982 after which all PJIs posted off parachute duty retained the additional pay if remaining 'appointable': medically fit and willing. In this matter PJIs, therefore came under the same provisions as all other RAF flying branches.

As my own PJI service lengthened I came to puzzle why these anomalies had persisted. In 1972 my deputy Ken Kidd was detached from PTS to be a specialist advisor to an RAF-wide study of job description. The eventual conclusion that PTS work had little in common with main-stream PEd work, and should be separated, was unsurprising to PJIs. Sadly, suggestions like this were not be supported by the policy branches, however logical they appeared.

Away from high politics, of course, most PJIs just got on with the job, together with their personal fitness and sporting interests. A survey at any time in post-war PTS history would have shown participation in every sporting activity possible: shove ha'penny to offshore yacht racing; caving to men's hockey at Olympic level. (One man was reputed to have kayaked 'down Everest'.) The team games, particularly rugby union, absorbed the interests of many and John Mace recorded that in 1974 thirteen of the victorious RAF Abingdon rugby XV that won the Inter-Station Cup [yet again] were PJIs.

Any military unit whose primary purpose could be described as daring risk-taking will attract individuals whose philosophy is similar. During the Ringway days PTS quickly established a reputation for bold but safe achievement of the aim and this continued into peacetime.

After the war PTS became the only such unit in the RAF – No 1 Parachute Training School – and as a result somewhat 'tribal' in nature. PJIs were recruited (from another not-very-big tribe), trained and employed initially only by PTS, but frequently proceeding to other not-under-PTS-command duties, mainly in trials and procurement.

The Ringway boys' exploits had become legendary to successive generations of PJIs who, in the time-honoured traditions of all apprentices, had to earn their spurs before being admitted to the junior ranks of the family: they in turn fostered new mythology.

Thus the 1960s generations of PJI – joined an unofficial but quite strict crew room hierarchy of four levels: The Old, Old

Boys; The New Old Boys; The Old New Boys and then us: The New, New Boys. Such, occasionally provided interesting (with hindsight) and frustrating obstacles to individual progress in the new skill.

Naturally, the PJIs who had become the cornerstone of this repute were, for the most part, lively characters whose frequent cavalier attitude to peacetime's, more cautious norms must have caused the authorities some disquiet.

Parachuting incidents galore embroider PTS legend: riding bicycles out of balloon cages; PJIs 'accidentally falling' out of aircraft to see if the despatcher parachute would actually work, but it is the men involved in all of this whose deeds both terrified, puzzled but yet inspired each generation of newcomer:

The Drop Zone control party has been carefully placed along the landing-line of the trainee parachutists. The Flight Sergeant shouts for all instructors to double in to the Drop Zone Centre Signal. They arrive panting. 'Okay, lads,' says the Flight Sergeant, 'spread out.'

Ron Smith told of one occasion when the PJIs made their feelings known:

Instructors were used on fatigue parties – carting coal about, painting around the Camp. We didn't think much of it. One morning the fatigue party was told to make up an instructors' stick [a group of parachutists]. We did. We loaded ourselves with buckets, spades, brooms and dustbins, and when we jumped we lowered them below us during the descent. Caused chaos on the Drop Zone.

Dick Mullins remembered one PJI elder who terrified most on first meeting:

Jock Fox was for a long time the Parachute School's Warrant Officer ... [and] operated mainly on his own interpretation of any applicable rules and regulations ... once, when overseeing the weekly Station Commander's dealing with airmen on charges, Jock was heard to give instructions for the escort. 'March the guilty bastard in' – no thought given to "innocent until proven guilty".

Thereby the PTS ethos was established. Successive post-war RAF management was often given 'interesting times' on occasion; doubtless that still applies in the new century. Peter Watson, Officer Commanding PTS at the time, recalled an anxious moment or two during an extended visit to PTS by the Chief of the Air Staff who made a successful parachute descent into the sea:

Sir Peter, elated with his experience of parachuting, was keen that his wife should try some sort of descent, so it was agreed that she should make a tandem descent a few days later.

Came the day, in glorious weather I was there [on the DZ] with the School Warrant Officer, the Station Commander, his wife and the great man's personal staff: quite an audience.

With Steve McBrine as the tandem master everything went superbly: lovely exit, faultless descent and Steve brought them in, in with perfect accuracy. It was a beautifully light landing, right in front of us, but as Steve stepped forward they both pitched forward in slow motion ... Steve landed right on top of Lady H, albeit from the rear.

He quickly released her, and asked 'Are you OK, Ma'am?'

'Yes, I'm fine thank you, Flight Sergeant.'

'That's good, because for a moment, I thought we were going to have to get married!'

There was stunned silence ... everybody looked at Sir Peter.

'Ha, Ha, Ha, very good, Flight Sergeant,' said the great man.

We all relaxed, but for a moment we knew exactly what the colour of adrenalin was.

During one of my PTS tours a group of PJIs was placed under command of a non-PJI officer for exercise purposes. The young man struggled to make contact. The boys were not disobedient: like all PJIs they just needed to know who to hit next. Later when their leader plaintively complained, I could only console him by suggesting that sometimes it was not easy and I wore the same badge too.

George Sizeland (in my PJI infancy becoming one of the legends anyway) recalled his own early service in the company of two Old, Old Boys:

In 1950, I was working at the 16th AB Div (TA) [Airborne Division Territorial Army] in London. In those days we wore uniform all the time, mainly because civvies cost the sort of money that we never had. One day Lofty changed into the most immaculate, tailored, hand-stitched perfectly-fitted suit which I had ever seen. Lofty had gone to the best tailor in the East End, chose the material, was measured and paid the deposit. He then attended for the fitting, but never returned to collect the suit. Months later, at Sale Time, the suit would be in the window at a greatly reduced price; in post-war London there were few men the size of Lofty. So a friend would go in and make an offer, well below the sale price. The tailor would *be glad to be rid of the suit, and Lofty became the best dressed PJI at PTS ...*

Lofty's military parachuting career pre-dated PTS. He was one of the ten Fabric Workers from RAF Henlow who volunteered to become the very first PJIs in June 1940; an Old, Old Boy before the title had been invented.

George continued with another legendary tale:

I never knew Trigger's real name at Upper Heyford [the first post-war home of PTS], as I was still a Corporal PJI at the time, and by the time I became a sergeant he was known simply as 'Trigger'. Apparently he got his nickname after a taxi brought him back to the Mess from a drinking session in one of the local pubs. Considering that he had been overcharged, he staggered to his room, found his Service revolver, which he had 'forgotten' to hand in a couple of years previously and fired a few rounds at the departing taxi ...

It could be difficult for New, New Boys to leave any sort of mark in such folklore. Successive generations did their best, of course as they worked their passage from New, New to Old and finally just Old (this latter personally realised with something of a gulp). By the mid-1970s, however, the old titles were rarely heard (as was singing on the transport by the troops after their first jumps).

For the New, New Boy, learning to parachute skilfully was often the least steep of the learning curves as David Cobb recalls:

I was brand new and ready to march past OC PTS with my newly-qualified course. I forgot to give the 'Quick March' and arrived at the corner of the PTS Hangar ready to turn smartly to the right and along to Gerry and other important PJI

Officers on the saluting dais. At that point the then School
Warrant Officer, Pat Moloney [a New Old Boy by then, I
fancy] caught up with me and said something along the lines,
'Excuse me, sir but the troops only go with you if you tell
them'. What he really said is between him and me but, believe
me, my version is far more polite...

Dave confesses that he was never much good at drill anyway and
that attempt gave strong motivation to move to a part of PTS
where there was little requirement for parades – he became the
display team leader for the 1970 season.

All new PJIs quickly learned that every job at PTS had to be
tackled immediately and with panache. Grahame May recalls an
early attempt to impress:

[During] the six-month probationary period following
qualification I performed my duties with eyes like saucers and
ears like Dumbo the Elephant, trying to pick up snippets and
hints from the 'old and bold' ... on a night parachuting
programme I was confronted with a baby Para rolling around
in obvious pain after landing ... the medic diagnosed a
sprained ankle. However, he couldn't raise the ambulance by
radio so myself and a very experienced PJI were ordered to
double off to the RV to sort it out.

When we reached the Land Rover ambulance the driver could
not immediately be found so we decided to drive it [onto the
drop zone] ourselves where we were told to get the poor lad off
the DZ soonest ... We picked him up and threw him feet first
on his back onto the stretcher in the rear of the ambulance
and quickly slammed the doors. Knowing the programme
needed to get finished I drove off at a purposeful 20mph.
However, the parachutist's screaming in the back gradually

got louder and louder so naturally I drove slower and slower until on reaching the RV I was almost driving in reverse. We got out of the vehicle and, cursing the wimp, quickly opened the rear doors to see what the problem was ... it was only then that we realised that the poor bugger's right hand had been trapped in the door hinge ...

Together with fitting in to the PTS ethos new PJIs had to come to terms with a few army eccentricities. One such during the 1950s and 60s was a Teddy Bear that regularly attended PTS. It was the mascot of those Sandhurst cadets who came to PTS for training and was despatched on its first jump by Alf Card who had improvised a tiny parachute and harness. 'Twenty troops and one teddy bear to drop,' he advised the pilot. The Teddy was still attending PTS in the mid-1960s. Kip Gilpin remembered:

... for a number of years parachute training during a [Sandhurst] recess had been a popular activity. The club went by the name of its mascot, Edward Bear, who was an intrepid and regular participant in the jumps ... PTS considered it a sound exercise in Service relationships to run, concurrently, an Edward Bear course and a parachute training course of similar duration for Cranwell cadets ... During a well-planned night 'raid' Cranwell cadets stole Edward Bear ...

So, the PJI community was optimistically lively, especially in the face of poor weather. It could be tribal – rightly so – in its loyalties and was perhaps more sceptical of authority than most RAF units. It was indeed a curious one: at times maddening, yet the moment a posting-away occurred, individuals counted the days to return.

7.   FURTHER AFIELD

From the very beginning PTS was to work closely with the Army. The school owed its very existence to the development of a military parachuting capability: it was there that British airborne troops took their first steps on that road.

However, Maurice Newnham considered that a fall in parachuting confidence would occur when the newly-qualified troops returned to their bases after Ringway. He argued that this would be prevented by the presence of attached RAF instructors upon whom:

... they [the troops] had been accustomed to rely for the comforting assurance that the parachuting equipment was in perfect order ...

It appeared as a natural progression that once the troops had been trained and moved to their bases and airborne operations, PJIs went with them. They would fly as despatchers, but have an important role in continuation training and, before long, liaison activity. Some of this latter could be on the peripheries of parachute training; occasionally there was minimal connection.

General Gale had asked for Newnham's thoughts on 'keeping the chaps up to scratch from the parachuting angle'.

'I should like to see PTS instructors attached to the parachute units and accompany the men on exercises and operations,' Newnham replied.

Gale agreed, and quoted a joint War Office/Air Ministry directive that stated: Airborne operations are air operations and that the RAF is responsible for them until the men are landed on the ground.

This instruction appears to have led directly to the formation in late December 1941 of a new unit called the Parachute Exercise Squadron which assembled at Ringway but almost immediately moved to Netheravon on Salisbury Plain. We would recognise it today as the beginnings of that part of the RAF tasked to give specialised support to the Airborne Forces. PJIs from the Parachute School formed part of its nucleus. George Podevin flew on three sorties to Arnhem as a despatcher:

I was attached to 4th Parachute Brigade in August 1944 ... to assist with air training and despatching ... there were many other officer and NCO PJIs scattered throughout the Division...

George despatched (and jumped) on several big exercises in preparation for Arnhem, once with a padre who shared a bottle of wine after they had landed heavily on the edge of the drop zone:

Finally I went over to Arnhem as despatcher with the advance HQ Group on 17th September 1944, then on the following day with the main body ... The PJIs, their duty completed, returned to Ringway. I decided to stay and offer my services to the Poles ... [during their drop] the Poles really had a rough time ... we had a great deal of flack ... the enemy shot at the aircraft, at the troops [under their parachutes] ...

After dropping and escaping the ground fire the pilot's return to the UK base was handicapped by persistent fog. Lost in the fog and running out of fuel, the pilot announced his intention to ditch. George thought he would rather take his chance with the devil he knew, but while fitting his parachute a searchlight beam indicated land and an airfield:

... the pilot made a safe landing, declaring that we were at Plymouth. We were, in fact, at Manston in Kent, 138 miles off course and 250 miles from Plymouth ...

Norman Goodacre flew on the last big airborne assault of the war – *Operation Varsity*, the Rhine Crossing – during the despatch (in heavy flack) the American crew chief called 'All Out!':

I took his order to represent the English equivalent of 'Abandon aircraft. I was wearing an 'X'-type [parachute] ... I jumped and landed some 200yds from my stick on the DZ. This was held by the enemy, so having no choice, I went into action with the stick ...

When reading matter-of-fact accounts such as these it is worth remembering that not only were these PJIs not soldiers, they were not aircrew either – nor, at that stage, even honorary aircrew.

The development at Ringway of military parachuting techniques introduced a method of inserting agents by covert means to support the Resistance in Nazi-Occupied Europe. The records suggest that the ways of doing this by air were equally divided between short-landing aircraft and parachute. (In 2010 a newspaper obituary spoke of a wartime RAF pilot attending the 'SOE's jump school at Ringway'.) PJIs were involved with these 'clandestines' from the start: most as despatchers, but occasionally jumping too. Maurice Newnham recorded one such:

*Ian McGregor, one of the RAF instructors, volunteered for this
hazardous work [jumping into occupied territory] and was
landed by parachute on several occasions ... His gallantry and
the successful accomplishment of his missions gained him a
commission and the Military Cross ...*

So, and perhaps unwittingly, a new tradition was established:
the raison d'être of the RAF PJI was to work with the Army,
therefore, they had better live and work as closely with it as
possible.

These PJI elements living and working with the Army became
known as the PTS Detachments, remaining under command of
the home unit. This was to continue post-war throughout the
School's time at Upper Heyford, Abingdon and Brize Norton
until the early 1990s. The earlier arrangements clearly had
included PJIs going to war with their khaki brothers and this too
carried over into the post-war 'peace'.

British airborne troops were committed to a parachute assault
onto El Gamil airfield during the 1956 Suez campaign and RAF
PJIs were heavily involved in the preparations, as Stan Roe
recalls:

*[In Cyprus] All troops of 3 Para completed an intensive
synthetic ground training programme ... 720 troops were
trained [refresher training] in 72 hours ... because drop height
was to be 600ft there was no operational or safety purpose in
wearing the [newly-introduced] reserve parachute ... it was
agreed sodium flares would be used to mark the re-supply DZ
... The OC Detachment [PTS] suggested his staff were
eminently suitable for this task ...*

Stan and Don Birchley were detailed, and after a smooth flight,
left their Hasting:

... with a grimace to the despatcher ... the low drop height meant no messing about and the sandy ground came up quickly ...

Even under fire Stan took note of the PJI training:

... the standard of parachuting was good ... only one parachuting injury ...

Stan and Don then set about clearing the runway and preparing to receive the re-supply parachute drop which was accurate and successful. A French Dakota landed to pick up casualties and the PJIs sought accommodation in the damaged Air Traffic Control tower despite a strafing by a fighter aircraft.

So, RAF PJIs – neither aircrew nor soldiers – had jumped in with the first assault. (Similar frequently repeated deeds over the years receive no or scant mention in RAF history, but local Army commanders always noticed as Stan remembered):

Next day [after a cautious look-see and landing by a Valetta] a wing commander greeted the Battalion's second-in-command with a breezy, 'Shake hands with the first RAF Officer in Port Said.' The Colonel most courteously pointed out his slight error by introducing him to me. I continued as airfield controller ... until the RAF officially took over the airfield on 9th November. Four days had passed ...

Bob Roberts and Doug Fletcher joined *HMS Fearless* at Portsmouth on 5th April 1982 for parachute despatcher duties:

Tuesday morning saw Fearless sail out of Pompey with two blue berets among those lining the decks ... We obtained what maps of the Falklands we could ... it soon became evident that the terrain did not lend itself as a useable parachute drop zone

... When we explained that the Sea King was not cleared for parachuting, we were simply told, 'Get it cleared then!'...

The two PJIs did supervise some parachuting while at Ascension Island (the first ever static line parachute programme from a Sea King) but:

It was then decided by our masters that until we were required for parachute despatcher duties we would be employed as door gunners on the 845 Squadron commando-carrying Sea King Helicopters ... A few days out of Ascension, our task changed again. We were to meet up with a WO2 ... who would teach us the intricacies of thermal imaging ...

Even when going to war by parachute the troops' delight at evading mandatory parachute ground training could not be concealed. Roy McCluskey flew as PJI despatch crew over the South Atlantic:

The aircraft started its final run ... I felt my left elbow being grasped, and a very large, beaming Fijian face was pushed close to mine. 'Boss, this is the greatest joy of my life. I am parachuting into battle with the greatest regiment in the world – and Des Desbois hasn't caught me for synthetic training for three years'...

In peacetime many a PJI, working with the Army away from the PTS cocoon, would say that each day was war enough – a new crisis every time. One weekend in 1972 a small PJI team at PTS was called in to give immediate training to an Army specialist who was required to parachute into the sea. It was not refresher training, he was a non-parachutist and this and was to be a one-off jump. The morning's training went off all right (perhaps not entirely the trainee's view) and eventually the bomb disposal expert and his PJI mentor, Geoff Bald, boarded a Hercules aircraft at RAF Lyneham that afternoon. Terry Allen, a PJI permanently attached from PTS to a Royal Marines unit at Poole, took up the story:

When we were airborne ... was informed that somewhere at sea was a large ship with a bomb on board and that he [the expert] was to be transferred to it ... I discovered that his parachuting experience consisted of half an hour's ground training [it was slightly more] at Abingdon with Geoff Bald ...

Three Royal Marines would jump with the expert and, as the flight proceeded, the PJIs [Allen and Bald] prepared the party and their equipment loads to jump in two pairs. The aircraft approached the target in low cloud below the planned drop height of 1000ft and the PJIs agreed on behalf of the parachutists to come down to 800ft. During several orbits around the ship Terry Allen saw that the expert was beginning to 'look ill':

At 1930 the green light [signal to jump] came on ... we managed to get the first two parachutists out ... Captain X [the expert] was sick all over me ... We then started for the [second] run-in and I found myself supporting a very sick and nervous man ... just as the ship came into view the Air Loadmaster shouted 'Dummy Run!' [aircraft pass over the target without releasing parachutists] ... I shouted that we would never get him out if there were any more dummies ... the green came on. I forcibly ejected Captain X through the door. Lieutenant Y followed fast... We later had confirmation from the QE2 [the target] that all parachutists were safe...

PJIs on permanent detachment from PTS often joined their unit's exercises just 'for the hell of it' (and also to add a parachute descent to their annual requirement). As 'peacetime' regulations required PJIs both to despatch and form a DZ safety party on the ground, instructors making a personal jump usually joined the exercise without a training role. Gerry Delaney recalled such a scheme in circumstances far removed from the benign conditions found at the PTS training drop zone:

In the winter of 65/66, around late November, I and several others reported to RAF Benson. The name of the game was an escape and evasion exercise. After the briefing we emplaned on an Argosy aircraft and flew to Germany ... We started around 11-12pm for the drop ... it was so dark I could not see anything. Then I could hear men crashing into trees. Then I am in one myself, fortunately only a fir, so no damage done and managed to get the chute out of the tree ... Meeting up in the RV, handing in chutes and helmets, moving off in parties of three ... that night's distance was 18k, or was it miles? The search parties who were looking for us ... We could hear them smoking and talking – good give-away. I think we only stopped once, so cold ...

Occasionally the despatch crew would have a bit of fun at the expense of their parachuting colleague. On exercise with an Army unit in the Gulf a resident PJI offered to 'cover' DZ safety for me and I joined the jumping troops at the end of their stick. Mysteriously, as miles of desert drop zone rolled below my feet, I was held at the aircraft door for a 'final check, Boss' before being despatched in the usual safe manner. It was a long, hot trek to the RV, but, as I ruefully supposed, we had shown the troops that PJIs could 'take it'.

Peter Hearn recalled from his PJI youth a series of eye-widening experiences well removed from day-to-day parachute training at PTS:

... the Beverleys came lumbering in to fill the sky with parachutists ... as the aircraft engines faded, I watched silent men check their weapons, merge into groups and file quietly into the dusk ...

... in Denmark, with a powdering of snow, we shone Aldis lamps at the dark silhouette of a Hastings and watched twelve black blobs drift silently into the stubble field ...

... On York racecourse, on Newcastle's Town Moor, at Wormwood Scrubs ... on small DZs up and down the country, we dropped the Territorials from 'mobile' balloons ...

In 1973 Alec Jackson, an experienced freefall display parachutist and about to join a PTS Detachment, made an introductory jump with a patrol on exercise:

I was ignored as a nonentity – 'probably some effing blue job on a jolly' – until the 'Green' came on and we all poured over the ramp ... black dots all over the place, one or two spinning like tops ... but mostly OK ...

Alec had a near-miss contretemps at parachute opening height with one of the others and was roundly berated throughout while under his canopy. On the ground he was given no chance to introduce himself:

Then I saw him coming, obviously not intent on asking after my welfare . . I tried to interpret his enquiries: who I was; what was I doing; did I know anything about parachuting ... Given half a chance I could have explained . . hopeless ... eventually with a final mouthful of 'blue job wankers' he stormed off ...

'Welcome to B Squadron', grinned Alec's new and well-established PJI colleagues.

Alec also recalled that some months later he was working with the affronted trooper. They were *digging a sangar together up on the Omani Jebel* and laughed as they recalled their first meeting.

Any PJI would understand why an RAF Admin-branch man was learning how to pack handfuls of plastic explosive into the ground. All others would most likely rather not ask the question and pass quietly on the other side.

When Peter Hearn referred to 'dropping Territorials from mobile balloons' he was writing of what became a common duty for many PJIs. A Territorial (TA) unit would bid for a 'balloon weekend' so that they could maintain their parachuting momentum and in some cases complete the PTS 'wings' training when this had been disrupted by poor weather with one jump to go.

A balloon convoy of many vehicles – self-mobile winch, gas carriers and the like, usually duplicated – would arrive at a previously approved DZ and immediately set-up shop by inflating the balloon onto its temporary mooring. As Peter records, the drop zones were diverse: tight boundaries were common, but a sight-seeing public attracted by the hard-to-hide silver gasbag hanging in the sky frequently posed a greater problem. The troops would arrive throughout the weekend, often accompanied by their families and all intent on picnicking while the heroic men-folk did their stuff. A TA weekend could pose a stern test for the newly-qualified PJI tasked with DZ safety and despatching, especially if the weather was marginal for parachuting.

PJIs working on drop zones, and away from RAF (or Army) base units often found themselves utterly alone. Mobile phone technology did not exist and when things began to divert from the plan a potent mix of airborne initiative and quick thinking had to be deployed. This would often include back-tracking to the nearest red phone box and persuading the home-base switchboard supervisor to accept a reverse-charge call. If overseas the potential for further confusion was considerable, especially if international time-zones had to be crossed; the RAF aviators always worked in GMT, the Army in local. Whatever else happened and even when matters had been beyond their control, it was frequently the DZ Safety party who faced the first accusatorial questions.

Standing under a night sky anxiously searching for blossoming canopies – every parachutist had to be accounted for, and there could be a couple of hundred – brought a new meaning to solitude. You knew the doctor and his team was nearby, the aircraft had announced numbers despatched and its lights were still in sight, but tired eyes could play tricks. Very occasionally cascades of carelessly-packed equipment: water bottles, rations – on one notable occasion for me, a pistol – could thud all around. Most of us stood our ground rather than dodge about to avoid missiles that could not be seen anyway. Exercise loads under notoriously unreliable stores parachutes could pose considerable risk. Chris Thorn recorded in the unit journal:

For the DZ safety officers their task is seemingly becoming more hazardous. The dangerous part of their job always used to be driving around the country to the DZs. But Boss returned today having had a narrow escape ... He calmly watched the stream of Fat Alberts (C130 Hercules aircraft) approach and disgorge their one-ton loads. Directly overhead one parachute malfunctioned and curiosity turned to panic as the load seriously gained speed and headed straight for him. The Army officer alongside swore briefly and stumbled into a headlong rush for the (hopefully) safe area. The boss – still attached by his headset lead to the radio on the ground – was understandably a millisecond slower ... Ten feet away the store impacted at about 12.6 on the Richter scale ...

An appalled Chris had been watching from nearby. His Richter-Scale estimate was, perhaps an exaggeration, but the 1-ton cube almost exactly filled the space my army colleague and I had created between us. 'Bugger this for a game of soldiers,' the soldier said with feeling. 'I think I'll stick to parachuting, and I'm not too keen on that either.'

Bryan Morris recalled standing under an ink-black Libyan sky knowing that the aircraft had just dropped a Land Rover and trailer. Nothing could be seen and he supposed it would have been pointless to run. Eventually thunderous impact noises announced safe but still invisible arrival.

John Cole, newly attached to the Airborne Forces had a bad day:

... my first operational mission was to the Isle of Man ... The lead aircraft [of three] – by my inexperienced estimation – was too far seaward; suddenly I saw equipment containers being jettisoned in the stick from that aircraft. What the hell was happening? Hadn't they fastened their equipment correctly? ...

Things speeded up somewhat for John at that stage: 18 parachutists had gone into the sea and the safety boats were not afloat. Oh shit! Why me?' Meanwhile, the doc had the last word:

*...'I have been in Ireland for five months' he said. 'I have had several close calls but nothing closer than from a f****** crab who almost killed me without firing a shot or letting off an IED' ... After a period of what seemed like hours, everyone was safely accounted for, including the Company Commander who*

looked at me as if I was something who had crawled out from under a stone ... I became more nervous when the Quartermaster asked who was going to pay for the lost weaponry and clothing that had been ditched ...

A solitary PJI drop zone safety officer could arrive in advance of an exercise expecting the despatch team to 'catch-up' when they arrived with the jumping aircraft. His time could then be usefully passed in confirming that the DZ remained safe to use. Liaison with local support units (many not recognising the PJI breed) was also useful, as well as simply fitting into the scene. Bryan Morris, sent to Belize, described a routine 'day at the office':

... seemed we had a small detachment of troops down there whom, for reasons of their own needed to parachute on to a DZ yet to be identified ... The following morning involved meeting the troops, being briefed on what was required and being allocated a fully armed and heavily laden 'minder' ... Next was a meeting with a mad Parachute Regiment captain who somehow or other had arranged secondment to the RAF to fly Puma helicopters ... we set off south at high speed, low level to find a DZ. Only one appeared suitable and then in fading light we flew at treetop height, at max knots back to Airport Camp ... Early next morning, accompanied again by the minder and all his kit we set off once more in Captain 'X's' Puma to take a closer look at the preferred area ... and relatively easy DZ recce followed ...

Bryan now had a ' few days to kill' before his drop and innocently agreed to attend a local unit's adventure training camp:

... After being driven to the RV, I met a handful of the adventure-training instructors, all of whom had been on some *serious R&R in town that involved copious quantities of alcohol ... My accommodation was indicated somewhat offhandedly: a bleak, isolated and totally barren barrack room on stilts ...*

Suffice to say the [eventual] drop was pretty much routine and incident free. Albeit a score of jumpers had landed on the DZ, a mere handful joined the Puma for the return journey – wonder where the others disappeared ...

Bryan's experience was typical: several days journeying and preparation for a quickly-concluded, incident-free result. Sometimes the adventures endured upstaged the 'death-defying' parachuting and it was frequently best not to enquire too closely about why the Army wanted to parachute just where and when they so often insisted.

On parachute exercises there could be a tendency to include into the PJIs' remit problems that should more properly be dealt with by the support elements of the task. Consequently, and usually in the interests of getting the parachuting bit of the job done (having chivvied aircraft, troops and weather in pursuit of that), the PJI-on-the-spot could find himself taking responsibilities that strictly speaking were not his.

In late 1969 I was attached to an airborne gunner battery on exercise in the Gulf. Supposedly based on Bahrain, we had gradually migrated to a dusty RAF airstrip outside Sharjah. On arrival I sought to confirm proper reception for the parachutes coming on our aircraft the following day. The base engineering staff could not offer the storage conditions – temperature, humidity, free of chewing rodents – specified in their technical manuals. Uneasy about handling man-carrying parachutes, they declined responsibility. Only by me signing away their liability and finding a quiet corner to bed everything down could the exercise proceed. My army colleagues, whose HQ should have organised everything in advance anyway, dismissed the hiccup as 'typical Crab sideways shuffling', and was I not ashamed of my cap badge?

A PJI could easily pass a whole tour of duty on permanent detachment thereby posing interesting RAF admin questions if an Army formation took a PJI team with it and in turn split off a part of that including an individual PJI. Many of us caught in this potential administrative minefield tended to tell our non-PJI RAF masters of our adventures after the event and hope that nothing went wrong during the detachment-from-a-detachment-from-a-detachment.

Happily by the late 1970s the RAF personnel management system had come to terms with the Parachute School's strange demands and most PJIs moving to a PTS Detachment did so under formal posting instructions. Even so, it was difficult to account for PJI inclusion in every 'Army-inspired' movement at times, hence the occasional confession after the event. Of course, this could leave individuals very exposed as happened after one major demonstration parachute assault.

The Airborne Forces had been invited to commemorate their wartime beginnings at Ringway, and what better way than a medium-sized parachute drop in the presence of the assembled Airborne 'Top Brass'. The affair went only half-to-plan because survival demanded an abort after the first aircraft pass when the already-borderline winds rose well above limits. There were no incidents other than one trooper whose snagged parachute left him dangling, uninjured, down the side of a building. Typically, it was only pictures of that rather amusing scene, together with lurid headlines, that adorned some newspapers next day.

As the responsible PJI, I was summonsed to my RAF HQ to explain myself: why had I mounted an 'unauthorised' parachute display onto an international airport? And why was the Press there in such force?

Thankfully, I had my written orders that detailed the job as just another routine task in support of the Army. I had to concede that Manchester Airport was a little-out-of-the-ordinary as a DZ, but otherwise we were just doing what the Army wanted, a fact confirmed by the fulsome telephone congratulations I had received from the Brigade Commander. Similarly, my distant PJI CO, he too had served closely with the Army, wrote to say thank you; no doubt thankful that it had been me and not him out there.

When I arrived on the PTS scene in the mid-1960s Detachment work seemed not to every young man's taste, but by the early 1970s it was if things had reverted to normal and every PJI could expect to serve at least one tour of duty permanently detached from PTS and in close daily contact with an Army or Royal Marines regular or reserve formation. Detached PJIs appeared in the chain-of-command of PTS. Every RAF admin matter: personnel management, transport, accounting, equipment, et al was processed via a distant, occasionally torturous network and weeks could pass between visits to the RAF home base.

In late 1968 I was sent overseas to a parachute battalion 'for a fortnight' and returned four months later. During another tour nineteen years later, I reported my arrival to the Military Attaché in Jakarta. He was a cavalryman and conceded little knowledge of Airborne matters, but puzzled why the RAF could possibly be involved: especially as my team of three constituted the only other British military in Indonesia at that time.

During the summer of 1956 Ted Parks was:

... in Cyprus during the troubles and was in fact in the HQ 16 Parachute Brigade Group. The Brigade was ordered to cordon and curfew a troublesome village ...

Not too much PJI work so far, perhaps. Ted continues:

Moving from Nicosia I was told to travel in a Land Rover which was to be the last vehicle in the convoy up the mountain roads ... A vehicle ahead of me broke down where the road was narrow with a sheer drop on one side and rough mountainous areas on the other. The lorry driver said he could fix things in about thirty minutes, but after a wait I was told it was not repairable there. I then found a patch of land off the track where we could park the vehicle so that we could move on. You can imagine the problem parking a 3-tonner up a mountain track. But you know what Paras are. We left the vehicle and its crew, plus a few other soldiers and went on ...

On arrival [at 3.0 in the afternoon] I told the Brigade Major what had happened and gave him the map reference of the broken-down truck ... At about 9 o'clock I was tucked up in my sleeping bag when I was told to report to the Brigade Major. 'The lorry cannot be found and the soldiers need food. Collect an escort and go back to the lorry with this food.' ...'Yes, sir,' I said and off we went. We even had to drive through a British ambush ...

Not much to do with parachute instruction here and it is entirely possible that the RAF would rather not know that one of their officers was running an Army convoy up a mountain road. Any PJI would recognise the scene, however, and there were many occasions when we had to make a conscious effort to remember which service was actually paying our wages.

During the mid-1980s one of the PTS COs, wearying of having the School's work briefly summarised in 'Any Other Business' during the station commander's weekly 'state-of-the-nation' conference, decided to give greater detail. As well as the hundred-odd soldiery under training about the place, he detailed that morning the scattering of his PJIs about the world, many in places and doing things with army units best not mentioned.

As flies on the wall, Louis Strange, Maurice Newnham, and all PTS commanders since, would have relished the reflective silence that followed.

8. PUSHING THE BOUNDARIES

Arguably in the early days at Ringway, and until reliability improved, every parachute descent was in the nature of a trial. The same 'trial and error' philosophy probably applied to ground training too.

Many equipment modifications followed bitter experience and, of course, developing expertise. Others seem to have been imposed upon the school for reasons of material shortages or inexperience. Maurice Newnham made a pungent comment when recalling how he submitted a solution to an inherent fault in the parachute design of those days:

*The pundits at home lost no time in signalling their
disagreement with my request and I thought again what a pity
it was that the people who had assumed responsibility for
parachute design had never jumped themselves or shown the
slightest inclination to do so ...*

Of course that problem was solved eventually, as indeed were many subsequent, but Newnham's rather rueful observation would come to epitomise the everyday PJI's wary attitude to any interference with the parachute equipment they were using on a daily basis.

Post-war, as the future of military parachuting seemed assured, parachute design, procurement and use fell into the bailiwick of an occasionally uneasy triumvirate comprising the manufacturers who had goods to sell, the RAF engineers for whom parachutes became another bit of to-be-cared for equipment and the 'shop-floor' PJIs who simply wanted to jump with the things as often as possible.

Together with the technical imperative to improve things, perhaps it was the PJIs' insatiable desire to add a bit of spice to life, and also to get the job done, that gave impetus to 'trials' work.

Alf Card, another legendary figure to the 1960s generation, recalled from 1943:

Joe came up with his lop-sided grin and said that he was making a descent after my stick had been dropped. I then noticed that his 'chute was not your usual run-of-the-mill static line job. For a start there was a ripcord and he was also wearing a reserve. 'What's that?' I asked. 'A trainer main,' was the reply ... The pilot apparently knew all about it and didn't turn a hair when I told him Joe wanted to be dropped from 2000ft ... I had never been up so high before. It looked a hell of a long way down ... Later I found out from Joe that he had come across the 'chute in the packing shed and had charmed the SNCO in charge into letting him use it ...

Some PJIs confessed (usually well into retirement) to making 'unauthorised' modifications to their parachute assemblies; sometimes, it seems, just 'to see what happens'. In the days when they were seeking a cleaner, more gentle deployment of the freefall canopy by packing it in a sleeve Peter Denley re-called many a household 'Singer' being brought into service:

The two British parachute manufacturing companies were cautious about producing a sleeve, many a jumper's family sewing machine rattled late into the night. My first sleeve was made on my mother's sewing machine from a large Stars and Stripes ...

Officially, of course, trials work – Research and Development – was the remit of special units and from the very beginning one of these was the Airborne Forces Experimental Establishment (AFEE). Originally established at Ringway alongside PTS, then from August 1942 at Sherburn-in-Elmet, it moved to Beaulieu in the New Forest in January 1945. Its last move was to be absorbed into the aviation test unit at Boscombe Down in 1950 and where PJIs serve to this day.

Alan Brown, another end-of-war redundant aviator seeking continued service, took the PJI option and trained shortly after PTS moved to Upper Heyford. Following a call for parachute testing volunteers that had attracted no takers from more experienced men, Alan put his name forward as a New, New Boy. 'It was the best thing I did in the RAF,' he was to say later. 'Interesting work and not a lot of bull.' He recorded a parachute trial that took place before his time: it makes hair-raising reading:

In September 1944 a Barracuda torpedo bomber fitted with two strange box-like constructions under the wings arrived at AFEE. The boxes were called Cuda Floats, a false description to hide their real purpose, which was to drop four men ... The boxes were made to just hold two men in very cramped conditions with 'X' type parachutes and a minimum of equipment. There was no room for the usual AFEE reserve parachute for test work ...

Perhaps the most unusual parachuting idea was the way the men, cramped in the boxes were dropped. The pilot pressed a switch and the 'bomb doors' below the men's feet opened ... The tests followed the usual AFEE pattern with block dummies dropped from each position ... The PJIs of the Test Team then did a series of live drops from 1 500ft with the aircraft flying at 85kts in level flight ... tests continued until

*February 1945, and all were satisfactory, but the flights were
very cramped and had a psychological element …*

The record is unclear on whether the system was ever used in
anger, and an intriguing question remains: what 'psychological
elements'?

Brown also recalled trials of a barometric opening device for
manually opened parachutes.

*The first call for such a parachute came with the development
of bombers that could fly at 40,000ft or above. The worry was
that if the aircrew had to 'bale out' and they pulled their
parachutes at that altitude they would have to float down
slowly without oxygen. On the other hand if they delayed
operating their parachute until at a lower altitude it was
thought at that time that they might black out and not pull
the rip cord. This might seem strange today in an age of sky
diving as a sport. Now barometric devices are incorporated in
many modern parachutes.*

*The GQ design of 1946 had a barometric device which
established an electrical contact when the man had dropped
to, for example, 4,000ft. Two small batteries then fired two
.22-size cartridges in an exploder box situated lower down on
the harness. This blew out a piston enlargement on the lower
part of the rip cord which operated the release on the seat-
type parachute …*

*Five examples of the parachute were sent for tests at Beaulieu,
between 1946 and 1949, and an extended programme of
dummy drops were made from a Halifax from 10,000ft and
above with various barometric settings. There were a few
failures when battery contact failed to explode the charges,*

but these problems were sorted out. There are unconfirmed
reports that one live drop was made with the parachute ...

By the 1960s the 'trials' system was very well established with its own traditions. PJIs could serve in specialised procurement and trials appointments which, as in the Ringway days, were separated from the day-to-day work of PTS and its detachments with the Army.

The 'trials teams' would test-jump new equipments, reject some, further develop others and, eventually, issue a 'clearance' for use under stated circumstances and from particular aircraft: much as happens for all newly-acquired equipment.

That report could be passed on to another small PJI team – still separate from PTS – whose task was to translate the formal clearance into standardised drills and procedures. In turn a small team at PTS would write instructional manuals and standing orders and it was from these that the 'gospel' would be drawn for the trainees.

Occasionally PJIs from PTS would be invited to jump with the test teams towards the end of a trial: in the mid-1980s I enjoyed a couple of visits to Boscombe Down where we jumped the big military 'square' (ram-air parachute) that was being developed in static line version. Similarly, it was not unknown for large parties of parachute-qualified troops to act as 'jump-fodder' so that an about-to-be-cleared parachute could accumulate a credible number of descents before final clearance to service.

Peter Hearn visited Boscombe in the early 1970s to jump for the first time with the Para Wing:

... a device shaped like a paper dart, with uncertain opening
characteristics but a very positive forward speed ... in dense

cloud and a compass on top of the reserve ... I flew it [like]
driving a fast car down a foggy road, waiting for the crash ...

He also 'guested' during the trials of the 'stabilised fall' system. Intended to shorten the time needed to train an operational military freefall parachutist, this equipment was to offer automatic stabilisation during the freefall phase of the descent;

... burdened by the excessive weight and intricacy of the device.
At 9000ft I hooked up ... away I went with a normal
'statichute' exit ... the small stabiliser parachute took over,
and I was hurtling downwards at about 100mph in an upright
position. It was a most helpless sensation: I felt trussed, like a
bundle of stores, with nothing to do but watch the altimeter
unwind ... at 3000ft there was a sudden lurch ... and then the
big TAP [an advanced 'round' canopy of the day] took over,
and we were back to normal. No, not for me! ...

During the inevitably long development period of this parachute system simultaneous and considerable progress was made in teaching body control in military freefall and thus the need for such mechanical complications disappeared.

But not before claiming the life of one 'trials' PJI: Sergeant Les Hicks.

The 1946 barometric trial described by Alan Brown was destined to be repeated as the search for a reliable opener continued. 'Not everything worked', recalled Roy McCluskey:

In 1970 The IRVIN GB Hitefinder had just reached full user
trials standard. At that stage they were a precious resource
and could not be hazarded on the free-fall bundles [equipment
only] that were being investigated. The Czech-built KAP3
opener was far less reliable than the Hitefinder but was

*deemed reasonably safe to fit on the bundles ... sometimes
they opened high, and sometimes they didn't open at all ...*

*On one sunny October morning a KAP3 operated at about
15000 feet, instead of 3000 and the load drifted well out of
sight of the DZSO [Drop Zone Safety Officer] in a westerly
direction ... on the trundle back to Abingdon it was our keen-
eyed Parachute Regiment driver who caught sight of a gently
flapping canopy wafting over the world heritage site at
Stonehenge. The earnest duty guardian assured us that he had
done his Para course at Upper Heyford and realised the
importance of this bit of highly classified kit. We stuffed it
into the back of our Land Rover and scooted up the A308. So
yet another military scandal was kept away from the
voracious Wiltshire press offices ...*

*It was much more unnerving when the unpredictable devices
failed to operate at all. On one night sortie the aircraft radioed
to the DZ that eight troops and two door bundles had been
despatched from 25000 feet ... Usually the parachutes could be
heard developing overhead, but hearts stopped beating for a
while on that night when one item whistled into the earth
close to the DZ safety team. It was a particularly dark night
and it took some time before we could check the jumpers had
landed safely and that the plummeting load was only a bundle.
We never did find that dummy load of ammunition or its
parachute, which must have dug a very deep little cache for
itself under the turf of Salisbury Plain ...*

So, again not much personal parachuting for the PJI Drop Zone
team, but similar dangers to that faced by all on 'stores' DZs

Needless to say, despite exhaustive trials and comprehensive
clearances some equipment never caught the 'working' PJIs'

imagination and the worst of these in my direct experience was Mk5 of the greatly-trusted 'PX' parachute. The 5, or GP Harness, version brought along a more-simple-to-adjust harness (albeit made of less-comfortable synthetic webbing) under a standard 'PX' round canopy with the proven 'netskirt' anti-inversion modification. All of the latter was by the early 1970s very much part of the PTS 'reliability-never-fail' culture sold to the trainees.

However, where all previous static line parachutes had been permanently attached to their harness, the new one was designed to separate on demand. (Only on the ground, and for reasons that were never fully explained.) This was effected by a shoulder release device whereby the 'female' body that carried a spring-loaded locking peg released by a multi-jointed external lever received a 'male' lug that was the end point at each shoulder for the parachute canopy's rigging lines. That it takes such a complex sentence simply to describe the basics speaks volumes for my memory of the device. Peter Hearn, like all PJIs, was 'a great believer in simplicity of parachute equipment', but in his words, the shoulder disconnects on the Mk5 were 'disturbingly complex'.

It was, ironically enough, in Peter's company that I witnessed an early – possibly the first – failure of the device, by then on general issue. During a demonstration for a visiting politician the first canopy of the stick simply streamed, making no attempt to open. Happily, the parachutist got his reserve up immediately having, as he reported, seen the suspension lug come away from the harness as he passed through the door.

Thus began a long period of retrospection and 'think again', during which I was appointed away from PTS. On return three years later I found the Mk5 back in general use again but with few PJIs trusting the thing. One of a series of modifications served only to prevent the very action for which it had been intended originally: release of the canopy from the harness.

Nonetheless, the assembly survived throughout the 1970s and into the 80s and PTS had to find ways of deflecting the PJIs' distrust, which was being passed on to the trainees:

Swinging under the parachute – usually at too low an altitude for successful reserve deployment – one or other of the shoulder releases, about three inches from the end of the nose, would catch the eye and a fellow would take to wondering what was going on in that ill-ordered collection of springs and manufacturing tolerances ...

Lesser snags, especially if recurring during the relentless conveyor belt of PTS ab-initio training could be reported 'up the chain' with a request that the 'trials people' sorted them quickly. This often resulted in a visit from the team either to have a look, followed by a think, or to suggest an immediate solution. Whatever transpired had to be reduced to a written report and modification of procedure for PTS to continue 'legally'.

In truth, throughout the 1970s and 80s, the MK5 apart, there were few persisting problems, although a period of puzzling unlocking of the central harness lock – Quick Release Box – caused some head-scratching. One opinion was that over-excited, forgetful trainees were simply undoing their harnesses too quickly on landing.

PTS then suffered a spate of equipment loads being jettisoned by trainees during their descent. Although not involving real weapons and expensive kit (a PTS training load of a sand-filled jerrycan and a rifle-sized lump of four-by-two could still dent a DZ ground party) the reasons for letting go the load had to be found.

At PTS everybody swore that it wasn't a training omission, so the boffins at Boscombe Down scratched their heads again and subjected live jumps to slow-motion, stop-frame photography. The culprit, it seemed, was a newly-introduced synthetic strap. This fastened the load's suspension rope to the parachute harness, but tended not to 'grip' its metal buckle like the old flax one. The loose end would flap in the slipstream and, sometimes, slip free completely.

So the filming suggested, and the trials people came to PTS to say so. It appeared that a simple system, which had survived in its original form for two decades or so, had been confounded by the introduction of modern materials. The solution, we were solemnly advised, was an elastic band around the tail end.

Thereafter PJI despatchers would include a handful of the official bands in their flying kit.

It happened occasionally that an in-use snag would provoke a 'trial' ('suck it and see' again?) Bryan Morris recalled such an event when, after a consignment of rain-soaked parachutes had had to be replaced during a very big exercise in Greece, 'PJI verve' back in the UK instigated a trial to see if wet parachutes would work:

At the time, who knew? ... parachutes were subjected to a variety of 'rain': light rain for a long period; moderate rain for another period and heavy rain for yet another period ... memories remain of jumping in early 1964 wet parachutes from the balloon and aircraft. Apart from the noticeably increased weight of the parachutes and being drenched in water droplets as they snapped open all worked as they should

...

In the late 1980s when the Airborne Brigade began to jump with the new SA80 rifle those of us at the Aldershot permanent detachment had already received written clearances and procedures for jumping with the weapon from our 'trials' colleagues. It was something of a surprise, therefore, when snags both in the aircraft and on the ground became obvious.

It appeared that the rifle was not robust enough to withstand being strapped to a parachute harness or rolled over during a landing. Plastic panels broke off, sling swivels were not strong enough, muzzles filled with earth; it was a sorry state of affairs and the Army looked to us to 'sort it'.

Repeated visits by the 'trials people' did bring a remedy of sorts, but the weapon seemed not to be suited to parachuting in the way the Army wanted to carry it, that is ready for immediate use on the ground. Meanwhile, the PJI despatchers' temporary solution was to add sticky black bodging tape and 1200lb parachute cord to the elastic bands already carried.

Alan Brown's account of a barometric parachute opener meant for high-flying bomber crews reminds us that not all PJI trials work was concerned with equipment intended only for airborne troops. Jake McLoughlin – almost accidentally – got involved in ejection seat tests:

It was 1958 and I was casually looking at the exhibits at the Farnborough Air Show. "You seem to enjoy parachuting," said a voice. It was Sir Raymond Quilter, the 'Q' of 'GQ Parachutes' ... he went on to explain that he would like the services of a parachutist to carry out ejection trials at Woomera, South Australia on a 3-month detachment ...

Jake 'naturally' volunteered but omitted to inform his [PTS?] superiors. They must have felt very much 'out of the loop' because it seems that Sir Raymond went straight to the top and contacted Marshal of the Royal Air Force Sir Dermot Boyle with news of the new recruit to ejection seat testing. As McLoughlin supposed, the 'ensuing discussions must have been hilarious'.

Soon enough, however, Jake was officially, involved in the test programme:

It was planned to carry out two live ejections [from a Canberra] in UK in advance of the Woomera trial ... I had made a couple of free fall jumps from a helicopter with the actual parachute to check the harness for comfort - there wasn't any ... The Canberra was soon ready for the flight ... We were flying at 5,000 feet and 200 knots ... It was a great relief to arrive at the long straight run in ... The 30-second countdown seemed like a lifetime; I felt as if I were in front of a firing squad and wondered if I would hear the bang. As I sat there I wondered what I had let myself in for. I liked parachuting, but this was ridiculous. The seat felt like a dentist's chair with a live grenade rolling about underneath it.

On ZERO I pulled firmly down on the blind and was aware of being compressed into the base of the seat. I took a quick look downward under the low loose blind and watched the sinister-looking black Canberra fly on just a few metres under my feet...

Half way through the second somersault there was a severe deceleration while my main parachute opened. I had felt the seat separation during this time and watched it hurtle away from me ... With the restrictions caused by two parachute harnesses there was little else to do but sit there and check the wind and drift ...

A stand-up landing required no effort on a stubby corner of the airfield and my boss arrived looking more relieved than I felt... The engineers were pleased, Sir Raymond was pleased, and I felt pretty good myself.

By the early 1960s much of the trials work was associated with the long-awaited introduction of a viable military freefall system. PJIs, procedures and equipment were being honed to that end. Naturally, a few possibly unforeseen, potential problems that had come along did not survive PJIs' pragmatism. Roy McCluskey again:

All of the CAA [Civil Aviation Authority] air controllers in the region were taking gleeful delight in telling us exactly where and when the JSFTT [Joint Services Freefall Trials Team] had parachuted each night. Apparently they could detect the troops [in freefall] on their every-day radar: Another problem to solve. The team sought advice from the Radar Research Unit at Malvern. After a deal of head- scratching they suggested that the troops should be encased in Radar Absorbent Material (RAM). This was thought to be an answer until the team leader visited Malvern and was presented with a suit made of RAM that would have served as an overall for Michelin Man. I think that Malvern were a little put out when it was pointed out that the suit was not quite parachute compatible ...

Perhaps it can be said that much of this work came to a climax on 16th June 1967 when five PJIs jumped from a then unprecedented height in the UK. Peter Keane, one of the group, recalled the day:

We as a team [John Thirtle, Keith Teesdale, Les Hicks, Ken Kidd, Peter Keane] were tasked to evaluate the oxygen systems at altitudes around and beyond 40,000ft.

We carried out a series of jumps between 20,000 and 30,000ft from a Hercules C130, which had been stripped of all but the most essential equipment, before making the ultimate descent from 42,393ft over Salisbury Plain ... we opened at 2200ft AGL ... [later] found that we had broken the world group freefall record...

Sometime later Ken Kidd was asked what it was like to be in freefall for four minutes:

"Freezing bloody cold and your arms ache!" was his reply.

Naturally, other agencies retained an interest in the developments and indeed advanced high altitude parachuting quickly came to depend upon their findings. The trials team PJIs, 'ordinary' PJIs and PTS in general were over a period of many years fortunate to have a friend in a senior RAF medical officer who was both an aviation medicine specialist and an experienced parachutist.

There are many PTS anecdotes that include Alan Johnson's background work on behalf of PJIs – I was only one of many who benefited from his professional intervention. Here we learn of his research into the PJI's old friend, fear:

On several night sorties from 25000 feet, Doc Johnson and his medics wired up a couple of jumpers [trials team members] to measure blood pressure at various stages. He later took some delight in analysing the print-outs to show that even the boldest and most experienced free-fallers had moments of

what our American cousins term 'the pucker factor'. Alan
could see just when the subject's heart skipped a beat.

Perhaps surprisingly, most had just a flicker as the aircraft
wheels lifted off the tarmac at Abingdon. Heartbeats generally
then settled, but he could trace most of the prepare-to-jump
procedure. There was particularly, but perhaps not too
surprisingly, a leap in blood pressure in the 1.5 seconds
between pulling the handle at terminal velocity and the initial
canopy development. That same 'gulp factor' showed up on
the print-outs of even the most intrepid, experienced,
parachutists...

Of course, for those of us churning out the basic-qualified
paratrooper at PTS, such sophistication was strictly for the
'Skygods'; the advanced and highly-skilled PJIs of the trials
teams. Even so, it was always worth listening to the trooper's
opinion on the kit he was given to jump. A Territorial Army
NCO and I were checking each other's parachutes before
jumping with the Mk5, then at the height of its PTS distrust:

There's only one effing thing will cure this bastard, Boss, and
that's a bloody great nut and bolt ...

Not being a 'trials' PJI, it was difficult to come up with a measured professional response to beat that, but I filed it away for
inclusion in any future report.

9.   AND HIGHER

As part of a thrilling public display during the 1920s and 1930s parachutists had fallen free – pulling a 'ripcord' to deploy their parachute – and some of these daredevils had joined the earliest instructors at Ringway:

A welcome measure of parachuting expertise was added to the staff when a professional jumper called Harry Ward arrived at Ringway ... Harry had made his first jump in 1926, and in 1932 out of the Service, he had joined Cobham's Air Circus as a stunt parachutist.

Peter Hearn also recalled:

Competition jumping was born in 1929 when a barnstorming parachutist called Joe Crane suggested to the organisers of the Pulitzer Air Races in Philadelphia that instead of the customary exhibition jumps by a number of professional skymen, a 'spot landing' competition might attract more attention.

The notion that parachutists might have some control over where they landed must have been almost inconceivable to the PJIs at Ringway, and the record shows that 'stunt parachuting' had no place there: the PTS of the day was developing a means of delivering squads of armed men to the ground without stopping the aircraft. However, the notion of falling free before opening a parachute was not forgotten – after all, escaping aircrew had to do it every time.

Within a decade of the war's end PTS instructors began to experiment with freefall parachuting. One of these was Norman Hoffman. George Sizeland, a life-long friend, recalls:

He was a modest man who never claimed to be a pioneer. However, his enthusiasm, courage and expertise ensured that PTS gradually, and sometimes reluctantly, accepted that free fall parachuting may have some merit.

In 1954 Hoffman, together with five other PJIs, was selected to represent Great Britain at the World Parachuting Championships in France. He became a founder member of the British Parachute Association and became the first serviceman to be licensed by the Ministry of Civil Aviation as a civilian instructor. He needed a civilian certificate to pack and inspect parachutes and, in the face no official support from PTS, took leave to attend a packing course organised by the parachute manufacturers. Hoffman had come up against a mindset that certainly affected some elements of PTS until the early 1960s: an unexpected dislike of bold, semi-experimental progress at unit level (perhaps that is why Sizeland used the expression *sometimes reluctantly* – it is appropriate).

Unlike some other nations, British airborne troops (and PJIs) never serviced [packed] their own static line parachutes. A very reliable and well-trusted system had developed over the years and a servicing unit, separate from PTS, handled all parachute technicalities, including packing and minor repairs. Even after military freefall training had become common by the mid-1970s – introducing Ram Air or 'square' parachutes shortly after that – all military parachutists lined up before a jump to take their parachute from a technician. Exceptions were eventually allowed at PTS: PJIs of the display team and some advanced parachutists packed their own rigs, but still under technician supervision.

Despite these cultural obstacles PJIs like Norman Hoffman and others continued to operate on a club competition basis during their spare time. They won several competition titles and learned something new every jump:

I set a German freefall record from 4000metres out of a Dornier 27 ... Later at Thruxton we jumped from a Rapide at a height of 14800ft with a delay of 77seconds ... A month prior to the record attempt I had used a smoke flare strapped to my boot, and it worked fine. The fireworks firm made us two more for the record attempt. I wore one and Jake McLoughlin wore the other. Unfortunately, his burned very hot and was burning his foot quite badly. Jake claims that in trying to get if off in freefall he discovered how to carry out turns and loops ...

A fatal accident in 1957 denied them continued access to the military DZ at Weston-on-the-Green and it was not until the RAF Freefall Club was formed in 1963 that further use was permitted.

Hoffman was once described as an engaging mix of progressive curiosity and old-style barnstorming recklessness:

He was frustrated when it was necessary to cancel a parachute display and disappoint the spectators. So he devised his own method of wing walking ... stand on the wing on one foot, hanging onto the strut with one hand; 'I wore a smoke flare on the other foot and couldn't put it back until the flare had burned out. I used the other hand to wave to the crowd ... stopped wearing a chute because if I fell off – well' ...

The mid-1950s to mid-1960s decade must have been an exciting period for the young PJIs for, despite setbacks and slow official recognition, PTS was beginning to match many others around the world. So saying, at least one senior PJI foresaw:

... that if we [PTS] didn't begin to teach military freefall, the Army would teach themselves or find others to do it ...

Indeed, one can read in a recently-published memoir (2010) that in the early '60s the Special Forces were already quite advanced in their practical thinking and disappointed that 'the RAF' played no part in that. A military requirement to insert troops by freefall had not been established, but it would not be long in coming and PTS would need to react quickly to the demands of the Army. Meanwhile:

... [PTS] didn't look on freefall as a science: we didn't think of the body as an adaptable shape that would answer to the basic rules of aerodynamics: although we were acutely conscious of the law of gravity. Freefall was an art, and there was only one way to master an art – to learn from the acknowledged artists. In the late 'fifties, these were the French ...

Thus four PJIs found themselves detached for freefall training to the French Ecole Des Troupes Aeroportees at Pau. That group introduced, perhaps, the now long-standing tradition of sharing experiences in advanced parachuting with other countries and which led eventually to PTS meeting a military training requirement for high-altitude covert parachute delivery of small teams.

In the1960s PTS was also picking the brains of the Americans, who had been developing High Altitude Low Opening (HALO) parachuting techniques. Thus a small team of PJIs went out to

Fort Bragg North Carolina to complete the US Army's HALO training course.

Eventually the Central Staffs were persuaded to issue a formal Operational Requirement for military freefall parachute insertion; the necessary equipment would, it was hoped, be developed in parallel.

In 1966 a Joint Services Freefall Trials Team was established, to which the RAF appointed six men, and in 1967 the Ministry of Defence accepted that there was a requirement for military freefall and authorised continuation:

Snowy Robertson and Andy Sweeney were on hand to guide the troops who, for the first time in the UK made their initial jumps from 12000 AGL. And so, at long last, MFF training became routine for selected soldiers ...

When Peter Hearn and the others had returned to PTS from Pau they were hailed as 'instant experts' and soon set about building experience. They were given new equipment: parachutes that deployed with less shock, stopwatches and altimeters:

... of doubtful accuracy, designed for mountaineers. It was very nice but we thought there would be no harm in continuing to count as well ...

And before the new training task really got under way there was a display to give – in Australia:

... We stuck Union Jacks on our helmets, borrowed some ground crew white overalls and felt very dashing ...

Back at PTS new ideas on body position during freefall were tried. Those that worked were developed further and a stable, face-down attitude became the base position. To be avoided was a sequence of uncoordinated somersaults, tumbles and spins leading to a potentially disastrous parachute deployment. Peter Hearn recalls the difficulty of breaking away from the hunched pulling position taught at Pau to a broader, shoulders-up shape that would allow the parachute to deploy off the back without hindrance. Stability at that point was key and Hearn recalls being advised to 'stick your belly against your reserve, think of nothing else all the way down'.

So on my next jump I fell all the way from 5000ft muttering 'belly button, belly button, belly button', and it worked ...

There cannot be a PJI of that period who was not on a very steep learning curve, whatever his earlier parachuting experience.

During the 1960s it could be extraordinarily difficult for newly-qualified PJIs to make progress in freefall parachuting. On graduating as instructors they were appointed on probation to that part of the school involved with ab-initio training of the Army: (PTS continued to be heavily committed to a continuous stream of 'back-to-back courses'.) and there certainly seemed at times a reluctance to grant time for newcomers to 'pick up' a freefall descent or two.

Ali Macdonald recalled that the rules were simple:

... you put your name on the manifest at morning break and, at 1205hrs, having seen your stick of [trainee] troops out of the hangar, you made frantic dash to attend the briefing, get your gear on and rush out to the aircraft. Jumps one and two were completed in quick succession ... jump three was fraught with anxiety. Part of the deal was that anyone could go freefalling, but you had to be back in the hangar, properly dressed, to meet your troops on their return from lunch at 1315hrs. The

floor Chiefies [basic training supervisory NCOs] were
normally grumpy old non-freefallers and their threat was
always the same – return one minute late from jumping and
you would be banned from freefalling – for life! ...

There was also, sad to recall but typical of a small 'tribe', an ill-defined culture which had it that 'you can't jump at [say] 5000ft until you've jumped at 5000ft. If, as many of us were, a newcomer was over-conscious of such 'Old, Old Boy ethos, it took a determined campaign to break into advanced work.

Recalling the risks of being late for afternoon work if a lunchtime freefall jump went over time, MacDonald's rueful further comment aptly summed up the potential frustrations:

A 'dummy run' [aircraft not dropping on a pass over the DZ
and going round again] on that third lift could mean the
difference between being allowed to progress in the freefall
world or being 'dumped' on the 'floor' [basic training] for the
rest of your days ...

If a PJI was slow to develop freefall skills, his week off basic duties – often in poor parachuting weather – might give only two or three descents: four or five seconds of fall each time. For many of us the first not-very-well-executed exercise needed repetition at the same altitude simply just to meet the minimum standard for that stage.

Official recognition by the Service that PJIs needed to be trained in advanced parachute skills was badly needed. Such could grant PTS a manpower allowance that would enable release on rotation from the primary task for in-house freefall training. It happened eventually – early 1970s – but until then PJIs 'chased' freefall descents during breaks in basic training or when not assigned to a course. There were times when this latter seemed never to happen. And then the weather inter-vened. And we were assigned to an Army basic course again. And so the hesitant 1000ft steps continued towards the 'magic' jump height of 12000ft, which was as high as military parachut-ists were permitted to jump without breathing oxygen. Attainment might open the door to display team selection.

It is interesting to note that of the two classes of 1966 not one of the first – all eight of us – became a notable freefall PJI, yet the second produced within four years two leaders of the freefall display team.

The Hitefinder barometric parachute opener eliminated much of the beginners' struggles, so by the early 1970s not only was there a formal military freefall training requirement laid on PTS, but that reliable device allowed the school to put first-time trainees out at 12000ft. Secure in the knowledge that if not they, then something would deploy their parachute. Thus they had around 60 seconds of freefall time per descent; long enough even for slow learners of my class to get stable – eventu-ally.

Similarly, time was being 'borrowed' within the PJI training course to attempt – always subject to weather - a couple of introductory freefall descents for each trainee instructor: formalised in the late 1970s by inclusion in the syllabus.

By the mid-1980s a reliable military 'square' (ram-air parachute) – the GQ360 – was on issue thus allowing PTS to put first-timers out at 12000ft to 'fly' an advanced parachute that had to be skilfully handled from opening to the ground.

Also in this decade what had begun as 'fair-weather' pre-season training for the display team – to Cyprus, Libya and eventually for many years to Southern California – took on an extended role whereby newly-qualified PJIs could enjoy a concentrated burst of freefall training and jumping.

This in-house advanced training – for the Army too – was in the hands of PJIs who had qualified to a newly-recognised freefall instructor standard that took PJI versatility to new levels of competence.

As the military requirement of covert parachute insertion, day and night, took drop heights to well above oxygen level it again raised the question: if a PJI, held responsible for the oxygen welfare of a dozen troops in a darkened, unpressurised aircraft, is not 'crew', then what is he?

In 1972, it appeared that the medics caught up with this development in PJI professional life. In what seemed like the personal crusade of a local senior medical officer, many of us at PTS were subjected to enhanced medical examination – and found wanting. One newly-qualified PJI lost his hard-won specialised trade annotation completely – thereby becoming unemployable at PTS. One thing that appeared to save some of us was that we had already completed at least one tour of PJI duty.

Protests resulted in a not-to-be-misinterpreted entry onto individual medical documents, these latter detailing restrictions on permitted employment and duty circumstances. For me mild short-sightedness – I'd joined the RAF with it – meant nothing but low-level parachuting; default meant 'loss of badge'.

Crew room scuttlebutt had it that because more of us were freefalling at terminal velocity through several thousand feet, then something called the 'extreme flight rules' were being applied. Few knew what they were, but it was a memorable potential set-back to progress.

Clearly, the days when John Robinson, one-eyed since 1945, could talk his way into PJI service were over. He had already 'edged' his way into the Physical Fitness Branch – fount of all PJIs – so how to get into parachuting?

There was a regulation, meant for aircrew only that they could do two familiarisation jumps ... just possibly a junior medical officer [at John's home station] could be bamboozled ... issued me with a medical chit, 'fit parachuting' ...

At Abingdon in early 1959 all trainee PJIs were medically examined, but as Robinson had a 'fit parachute' chit signed by a medical officer – *who was I to go against the word of a medic?* – he continued without one and eventually became a highly experienced freefall and static line PJI.

In the late 1960s early 70s, however, as military freefall blossomed, PJIs – still resolutely listed as 'ground trade' – were required, it seemed, to meet the medical employment standards applied to test pilots.

Happily for many of us, the medical policy on corrected vision was changed, and from September 1974 we learned:

... there is no bar to the wearing of spectacles or contact lenses for parachute jumping, including free-fall [by 'experienced' PJIs] from altitudes below 12000ft ...

Too late for some of the Old New Boys, but a welcome step forward nonetheless.

10. JUMPING FOR JOE PUBLIC

Running parallel with the developing military requirement for high altitude freefall was the growth at PTS of display parachuting. It can be argued that the two disciplines complemented each other, and in PJI expertise terms became inseparable: a time-served display team member, typically three years, was well placed to convert to the higher qualification of freefall instructor. The display team had filled a deep pool of experience.

Display parachuting at PTS had its tenuous beginnings at Ringway: balloon and aircraft parachuting demonstrations for visiting VIPs. Some of the early instructors had been recruited from the 'barnstorming' days of public display; Harry Ward, Bruce Williams and Bill Hire being best remembered in PTS lore.

Those of us joining the school in the late 1950s and early 1960s heard many tales of 'displays', authorised and otherwise: riding a bicycle out of the balloon cage; followed by a fully-kilted highlander, bagpipes skirling; the immaculate 'stand-up' landing under a plain round parachute so beloved by the skilled.

Norman Hoffman, and others, had acquired hard-won experience in sport parachuting competition and this led naturally into display jumping. Peter Hearn recorded:

... The first RAF Parachute Display Team drew on limited sport parachute experience ...

Eight men pose rather diffidently in an old photo. Six of them are PJIs:

... Tommy Maloney, Norman Hoffman, Alf Card, 'Timber' Woods, Doddy Hay, Danny Sutton ...

They were responding to developments in basic parachute equipment and techniques together with a couple of questions that perhaps circulated amongst younger, more adventurous spirits at PTS:

... didn't high level [parachute] delivery perhaps offer some advantage over vulnerable low-level dropping? ... would the display to the public of this dramatic aerial activity perhaps have some recruiting and publicity value? ...

And so it did, but the PJI's primary role remained that of training and development: they fitted in display practice when they could and as they learned new techniques. The record suggests that successive displays – usually at weekends – actually became a rehearsal for the next; a form of learning-on-the-job, perhaps.

Peter Williams led an early display in 1960:

I wasn't over-experienced. This would be my eleventh free fall.

The Station Commander took them to a spot of grass between the control tower and an enormous hangar surrounded by a parked flock of aircraft. 'That's where I want you to land,' he said. The team demurred a bit: the regulations (such as they were for displays) required a clear area 400 yards square. 'Damn shame,' muttered the Group Captain. 'Understood you chaps could land anywhere.' The team got airborne:

... the cloud base was 2800ft and the drizzle steadily coming down ... My altimeter told me we were either at 3500 [feet AGL] or 1500 according to the milled edge that changed the height each time I moved. Splitting the difference seemed to give us a reasonable drop height ... In the five seconds of free fall I vaguely remember catching a glimpse of someone's chalk bag [used to give a visible-from-the-ground plume] hurtling past minus its owner ...We opened in cloud ... with feet up, skimmed over the hangar to arrive amidst Jet Provosts, people and concrete – on or alongside the Station Commander's piece of grass ... I was grabbed by a beaming Station Commander who pumped my hand, 'That's gamesmanship. Said you couldn't land here. Just having me on, eh!'

So the scene must have been set for many future parachute displays: tight DZs (think Hong Kong, Horse Guards Parade); marginal weather (often so for any parachuting) and a thrill-seeking public to satisfy.

Peter Hearn recalls the exploits of the 'Big Six' who, in the early 1960s, left the aircraft in a linked group, tried not to kick each other too much during the freefall and, after separating for the 'pull', descended under a modified round canopy. This had panels removed through which 'escaping air' gave forward drive therefore increased control over their fate. Until then the actual individual's landing spot could be a matter of chance. At a Farnborough display a combination of wind change and poor communications had the team well short of the DZ, thus well out of the public eye:

Snowy Robertson and Stan Phipps landed in the high-security compound, which they were forbidden to leave because they hadn't signed in.

With hindsight the record suggests a great deal of 'suck-it-and-see' – nothing new for PTS/PJIs there – but things did improve quickly. Sport parachuting, away from military aviation, had shown how the aircraft could be 'spotted' to an accurate parachutist release point by an experienced jumper using known or forecast winds:

In military freefall we weren't allowed to do that. When we dared to suggest it we were reminded brusquely that telling pilots which way to go was the job of a navigator, not a parachutist.

However, such heresy became routine during the 1960s and accurate display drops resulted from the combined efforts of the crew flying the aircraft, the PJI 'spotter' peering out of the back and a ground party far below giving plotted wind information.

The excitement could be heightened if the PJI 'spotter', despite considerable freefall experience, was also learning the art, or just having not-too-good a day:

At 12000ft Stuart occasionally became a little belligerent in the thin air. The crewman's smoke pot [held in the slipstream to mark the aircraft for the crowd] had been a little slow so Stuart had offered boisterous help. Knocked against the doorframe the thing fell into the compartment … the team thought it best to leave at once.

One highly-experienced PJI was credited with developing a plastic plotter on which the wind angles could be marked on a rotating protractor and then cross-referenced to a distance/angle/height table to give a vector:

These calculations on the ground were in the hands of our
regular DZ NCO – Ron Ellerbeck. Ron did more in those days
to get us onto our DZs than our parachutes did.

Thus the DZ party measured wind speeds and direction at
1000ft intervals from the parachutists' ground target to as far as
a rising meteorological balloon remained visible through the
lens of a surveying theodolite. Combined with a recent forecast
of upper winds, the potential freefall drift, together with that
under the opened parachutes could be calculated. All this was
passed by radio to the aircraft which would be flown upwind to
release the jumpers at a point where success was achievable.
Even this simple task could stretch the sinews on occasion:

When I released the inflated balloon, instead of sailing
gleefully into the sky, the bloody thing simply gambolled along
the ground like a rebellious beach ball. From the team's point
of view – waiting to board the aircraft across the runway – it
meant that by any drift table they cared to consult the wind
with us must be at least 50 knots plus ...

In early 1961:

... we were told that we were to be formally recognised as the
Royal Air Force Parachute Display Team. No additional
instructors, however, would be established for the task: we
would have to fit in with our trials and our training roles ...

Their first official display was to be at the Farnborough Air Show
that September. Peter Hearn recalled concerns over the limited
manoeuvrability of their parachutes when jumping into 'tiny
DZs surrounded by expensive [aircraft] prototypes and expensive people'. Authority relented and new parachutes were
ordered. Although essentially still the standard 28ft 'X' type

canopy in use since the Ringway days, those for the team had been modified with a 'TU' cut-out that:

... doubled our forward drive to a heady 6mph, thereby raising our margin for error over the opening point [at around 2000ft AGL] from 200 to 400 yards. It also increased our rate of descent to a bone-rattling crash ...

After 1961 matters seemed to accelerate for display parachuting by the PTS team. Towards the end of 1963 an American parachute, the 'Conquistador' was provided: still a 'TU' cut but with a slower, more stable rate of descent and an increased forward drive. Best of all for public relations – a display team function from the beginning – was that the new canopies were in the pattern of the familiar red, white and blue RAF roundel.

This in turn was replaced by an advanced 'round' of the day when in 1965 the 'Para-Commander' or 'PC', also in RAF roundel pattern, brought to the display team 'potentially greater accuracy on small drop zones in higher winds'. Also in 1965 authority was given for a team leader plus six others to have no other PTS duties than display parachuting. The first leader wanted a catchy name for this new section:

A bird, it was quickly agreed, should lend its name to the Team. A spirited, fast moving bird ... 'Bird with a long glide on extended pinions, falling extremely rapidly' ... was the definition of the falcon. So, the Falcons they became ...

All of this gave the newly-qualified PJI of the mid-1960s a pinnacle to achieve in personal parachuting and for 1966 the record lists 17 PJIs associated with the Falcons. A display would usually involve 12 parachutists jumping at an altitude of 12000ft AGL, the numbers being made up by permanent 'borrowing' during the season of instructors from other PTS duties.

During this period a team member developed a tendency to upstage even the most extrovert of PJIs. Bob Souter, a junior member of the Falcons circa 1971, recalls an unusual additional task:

... Fred the incredible falcon – a real one, feathers, beak and all – was gifted to the Falcons by a sheik ... In 1971 the team leader said I seemed pretty good with birds so Fred was my secondary duty ... Fred did not fly too well with his lack of wing feathers, and we used to stick replacements in with glue as a temporary measure. In the summer we took him for flying lessons off the steps on the tower at Abingdon ... he would launch himself and glide down with a few flaps as I held a piece of meat ... one summer evening Fred missed the glove and, at 2ft above the ground, shakily went on and on with us in hot pursuit ... Reluctantly I reported the next morning that Fred had gone missing ...

Bob's search for Fred involved a deal of driving and eventually led him to South Wales where the bird had taken up residence in a policeman's front room. He returned in triumph and at that year's Battle of Britain Airshow:

... for once the Falcons were not completely the stars of the show. Fred was announced to the crowd as truly he had earned his wings ...

The bird would accompany the display team's ground party where, gripping its special perch resting on the Land Rover bonnet, it would sneer at the crowd. Sometimes it provoked extra duties for the ground party: placating angry parents whose children's teasing fingers had collected a sharp peck too many.

Bob Kent, who followed Souter on the team in 1974, also re-called being 'volunteered' as 'i/c the dikkie bird'. Kent naturally thought that he would be able to go on 'some sort of course to learn all about falcons, but officialdom said:

... 'Oh, we haven't we haven't got time for all that', and I was told just to chuck a dead mouse in the cage every so often ...

Unfortunately for Bob his bird was sickly and after a few consultations with a puzzled vet:

It seems that knowingly or unknowingly, our friends in sunnier climes had presented us with a dud ... some weeks later, I found that it had fallen off its perch and was as dead as a do-do ...

Here true PJI mettle surfaced. Anxious that human incompetence had killed the mascot, Kent arranged for a post mortem, but how to get the corpse to London Zoo?... [The vet] *told me to wrap it up in a brown paper parcel and pop it in the post. This threw me for a while until I realised he was serious, so that's what I did ...*

Things must have worked out for the two Bobs, despite their avian misdeeds: both went on to serve full tours as display team parachutists.

Display parachuting is no less affected by weather than any other. To achieve a sustained burst of pre-season training (and eventually winter freefall training for potential team members and other PJIs) it became the norm for PTS to seek fair-weather: Cyprus and Libya being a frequent location. 'Ordinary' non-'SkyGod' PJIs serving with the Army would occasionally come across the Team on one of their DZs:

We had been working in the desert for some days and on return to El Adem [Eastern Libya], looking like a latter-day Long Range Desert Group, came across the RAF Falcons

newly arrived and lolling about in their zippy suits drinking
ice-cold Coke ... I was in no mood for Lawrence of Arabia jokes
and viewed their pressed jump overalls and after-shave scents
with some scorn ...

In truth these overseas detachments provided a concentrated burst of uninterrupted freefall parachuting – three or four jumps a day easily possible – with a dedicated aircraft in attendance throughout. Such training prepared the newly-appointed team members for what by any definition would be an arduous display season: working weekends – always Bank Holidays - ; sometimes three displays a day at different locations; difficult, tight drop zones; relentless parachuting discipline and on-base continuation training in between. It wasn't always glamorous despite the 'working PJI's' scorn.

In1975 the PTS 'fair-weather' freefall training venue became a US Navy range on the edge of the Southern Californian desert close to the Mexican border; it was to remain so for 30 years The set-up was the same: potential team member training and development; general PJI freefall training, all out of the same accompanying aircraft. Ali MacDonald, then a tyro freefaller – a 'Sewer Rat' – was included in the very first detachment to El Centro:

We were taken to our accommodation and en-route had the
'chow hall' pointed out to us ... we piled out of the bus at a sort
of two-storey building that was situated all on its own in the
middle of a patch of desert and we looked around vainly for
our 'apartments' ... reveille was called at 0600hrs and the
serious business of learning to freefall began. We, the
students, were using the very basic PB1Mk5 round main
parachute ... those of you modern-day jumpers who might
consider that not landing in the intended target area is

somewhat 'uncool', let me assure you that unless you were first out of the C130 and the 'spot' was absolutely perfect then there was not a hope in hell of landing anywhere near to the prepared landing area ...

The generally ideal weather – cloudless skies, light winds – made for rapid progress in freefall skills. MacDonald recalls:

... on the very first deployment we only had nine available jumping days and we students completed 26 descents while the instructors and the display members had two extra jumps each day, but even that relatively low amount was far in excess of what would have been achieved in the UK in mid-winter . .

Ali went on to a 3-year tour as a display team member (followed three years after that as Team Coach), but first he had to survive a steep learning curve:

... hooked my PC [display parachute of the day] round into wind just as I was approaching a gap between the rows of cars and closed my eyes. This was going to hurt ... I came to a sudden stop ... suspended about a foot from the ground ... my parachute had passed backwards between a set of rugby posts ... hooked over the crossbar ... this Falcons parachute display jumping was getting serious ... behind me, stretching into the distance, were another hundred or so cars ... I had been display jumping for less than two weeks and so far my aircraft had been struck by lightning and I had nearly hanged myself on a set of rugby posts ... things could only get better ...

Of course, the introduction of any new parachute equipment to PTS frequently involved a deal of adjustment to techniques, procedures and, sometimes, long-held views. On the way out to the December1977 El Centro detachment the Falcons took delivery of their newly-authorised 'square' parachutes. Bryan Morris, the first PJI to be appointed as Display Team Manager for two consecutive years, recalls some of the problems encountered:

... tales from the jumpers of ultra-hard openings, and limbs and bodies being quite badly bruised. Also the PARAC [a formal reporting procedure to HQ] soared as many malfunctions necessitating reserve use were experienced – as many as two or three a day ... In those days use of a reserve automatically triggered a PARAC ...

Working towards a solution included a visit by a representative from the American parachute manufacturers. At least it gave the PJI team something different to think about:

... I believe he was a former 'Golden Knight' [the US Army Parachute Display Team], anyway a typical, possibly Texan, American: slow speaking, dressed entirely in an immaculate denim three-piece suit (we'd seen nothing like it) topped with dark glasses and a wide-brimmed hat ...

I too was on that detachment and although remembering the Team's concern, I missed the Texan. In any case, having made a belated entry to freefall parachuting I had problems of my own: long, lonely walks to the target from my landing spot, nursing my own bruises and enduring the entirely appropriate scorn of my more skilful, longer-experienced colleagues.

The El Centro detachments went from strength to strength: extended from nine jumping days to 14 and more; repeated as a pre-season training detachment in the spring and, in the mid-1980s, introducing freefall students to the delights of the ram-air parachute, which, if handled properly delivered him lightly onto his feet right into the target circle: a feat that had taken our ancestor parachutists years to master.

As formal freefall training for new PJIs became a professional requirement, so to attend an El Centro detachment followed and most newly-qualified PJIs aspired to become display parachutists. A three-year tour on the team – the norm by the early 1970s – provided a strong base towards PJI freefall instructor qualification. This would take them into advanced work with the Army, although always leavened with the original 'basic' work. Some would return to the team as Coach, a key appointment, others would return to basic PJI duties but in a supervisory role.

Yet others would move into a branch of parachuting that was new to PTS, but which had developed from the nation-wide growth of sport parachuting during the 1960s.

The British Parachute Association was founded in 1961 and rapidly began to coordinate standardisation and regulation of the sport. One of the Association's early executives was Bill Paul, a former PJI, very much an 'Old, Old Boy' to the 1960s generation.

The RAF Sport Parachute Association began with close links to PTS and its PJIs and it was inevitable that the School would take on a management responsibility. John Robinson recalled:

Free Fall Parachuting became my hobby, as sport
parachuting, as well as my salaried job. The Joint Services
gave me the opportunity to parachute from up to 25000ft ...
two minutes in freefall is quite sumpt'n ...

Connections in the sport parachute world seem to have given John an entrée to parachuting with the Army that, strictly speaking, could be described as non-military (or at least not within the remit of PTS):

Having spent a couple of years as RAFLO [RAF Liaison Officer] at Depot the Parachute Regiment [another of the Parachute School's far-flung commitments] it was not unusual to be invited to jump with the Red Devils Display Team. If I landed near the cross at a demo, I used to put on my blue RAF beret, if too far away I'd wear my red Para Regt one ... [Wearing of the Red Beret by some PJIs permanently attached to the Airborne Forces was another curiosity best kept at low profile in RAF circles.]

In May 1969 the Red Devils organised a training session in Germany prior to the British Nationals. John Robinson again:

The Sergeant Major of the team invited me to go with them, but there was the difficulty of getting away. Certain elements in senior ranks of the PJI world were, let us say, not too friendly towards the Red Devils Display Team. It was all Falcons and no fraternisation ...

Happily, and so no doubt saving John's continued good relations with his home unit:

That year the RAF Sport Parachute Association won the Accuracy and Overall groups in the British Nationals ...

By the mid-1970s parachuting had become one of the activities listed in the Joint Services Adventurous Training Scheme with Weston-on-the-Green, the Parachute School's long-standing training drop zone, becoming a base. The light aircraft used in this work eventually became a public provision flown by Service pilots appointed to PTS.

Curiously, there is little in Canopy Club anecdote about PJI involvement in this work or in the Sport Parachute Association.

What is clear, however, is that the fast-paced advance of parachuting techniques and equipment, in some cases led by developments in the sport, resulted in multi-qualified RAF PJIs who were highly experienced in every aspect of military parachute instruction; including flying as crew, at low and high altitude.

The Falcons, the Royal Air Force Parachute Display Team, *representing some of the finest military parachute instructors found anywhere in the world,* came to have their own distinctive jump suit, a glossy brochure and their very own groupie who pursued them relentlessly. They would frequently be as prominent on an Air Display Day bill as the renowned Royal Air Force Red Arrows Aerobatic Display Team.

Not bad for a bunch of ground tradesmen and admin wallahs.

11.   MILESTONES?

Parachuting must top the list of lonely and intensely personal activities; even sex, as we used to joke, should have at least one other in contact. The moment the individual passes through that aircraft door, at any altitude, they are entirely alone and potentially beyond help.

The rule is not absolute: there are legends aplenty of descending parachutists catching hold of a comrade's streaming 'Roman Candle' canopy and holding on for at survivable landing. Freefall instructors, 'flying' alongside trainees 'frozen' by fear have been known to reach in and pull the ripcord. In low level military parachuting there is a British procedure and equipment to retrieve to the aircraft a parachutist trailing behind at the end of his static line. And in modern times 'tandem' parachuting is common.

Survival depends upon an exotic blend of reliable equipment, faith in that and, perhaps most of all, a large dollop of self-belief amply reinforced by high-quality training.

PTS and its PJIs have been soft-selling faith - best described as trust – and self-reliance since the earliest Ringway days. The new recruit to the business quickly came to trust the instructor who in turn trusted other, more experienced PJIs. These latter presented themselves as the best instructors in the world teaching the finest troops in the world, using the most reliable kit in the world:

So keep your feet and knees together, and Bob's your uncle...

Every military rank was treated alike; the PTS ethos demanded nothing less:

At PTS we had one great truth to offer the sceptics – and some seemed to persist – after suitable training the Prince of Wales had to step out at our command. At that point there would be no return ...

Simply making a first parachute jump was for most a major milestone. PTS received many visitors who displayed a fearful fascination with the whole business of making a jump – just one. PJIs tended to make light of their work; parachuting an everyday event, but each one a potential milestone. In this light, could any PTS event become a unit landmark?

One or two in my chaotic archive catch the eye.

The1966 generation of trainee PJIs was somewhat awestruck to hear of deliberate parachute descents into tall jungle in the Far East. It seemed unlikely that anybody could forsake the flat lawns of Weston-on-the-Green to jump into an area beset by two-hundred foot trees. Only later, after reading matter-of-fact accounts, could we add the possibility to our new professional lexicon: a personal milestone that opened our eyes to the range of activity we were entering.

Dick Mullins, one-time leader of a rescue team, reported such an event:

It was decided that the drop [to a crashed aircraft site] would be made with the helicopter running in a westerly direction using the wreck as a dropping marker. The four aircraft were to remain in the same circuit at 800ft above ground level, dropping four pairs and then singles. Rendezvous on the ground was to be achieved by moving east and gathering at the wreck ... At o8oohrs the team was dropped east of the wreck: 10 going into an area about 300 by 50yds and two away from the main concentration to the south east. One parachutist was winded for about an hour, but otherwise there were no casualties; two came to rest in the trees upside down and six broke through the tree canopies and landed on the ground. Hang-ups in the trees varied from 200 to 150ft ...

Peter Williams recalled a personal 'milestone' in 1960/61: an attempt at a world record triple baton pass [actually a shaving brush] in freefall from 9000ft AGL:

Norman Hoffman said he would give the brush to Paul Hewitt and Paul would give it to me and a new world record would immediately be established ... I didn't want to appear inexperienced in these matters, so I pushed away visions of the world's Press interviewing me as the recipient of the Hoffman shaving brush and casually nodded my head as though it was something one did every day ... leapt out into a cold winter's evening ... only too aware that I was en route to Weston-on-the-Green without a helmet ...

At about 7000ft I was aware of somebody close and turned to see Paul, complete with shaving brush and pointing ... I gathered he was trying to tell me that I had lost my helmet, and I responded by holding my head ... whether or not he took it that I no longer wanted to participate in this world record shaving brush pass I couldn't say ... without further ado he cleared off; and so did the brush and my chances of stardom ...

I landed near the Winco's car [the PTS commander] ... My helmet landed near the Ben Johnson pub ... they let me carry the brush onto the coach, a sort of consolation prize, I suppose ... later that evening when I told Peg that I'd lost my

helmet doing a freefall she said, 'It's not like you to lose
things, dear,' and poured the tea ...

The PTS of the late 1950s and early1960s included much that
had been carried over from the Ringway days: dusty coir landing
mats; a crew room hierarchy that refused entry for trainee PJIs;
an occasional vaguely-expressed policy of 'you *can't do that
until you've done it'.* The place rightly boasted an unbeatable
record of excellence, of course, so why vary? Changes were
afoot, however, and perhaps these were hastened by the need
quickly to embrace new techniques, particularly free fall parachuting and its equipments.

My own first grasp of the new art was undistinguished:

*When I looked down to Weston its southern edge was just
passing under my boots. In an indecisive spiral of half-hearted
turns which gave the limited forward drive of the parachute no
chance, I continued my descent crossing some nicely ploughed
soft ground.... like a homing bird to its nest, I steered myself
without deviation into the upper twigs of a small copse ...
coming to rest in a hail of broken wood and outraged rooks ...*

It was a 'milestone' of sorts if only because in explaining myself
to the school commander – Gerry Turnbull, a Ringway 'Old, Old
Boy' – I achieved instant, if momentary elevation from the
anonymous crowd of 'New, New Boys. Matters did not improve
on my second attempt, but the despatching PJI did offer a last-
second tip: 'You're allowed to smile, you know,' winked Julien
Tasker, a Falcons team member of the 'Old New Boy' set.

Around that time I was detailed to jump onto Abingdon airfield
as part of a demonstration to a visiting VIP, with me was an
equally-newly-qualified colleague, David Gibbons. It was windy
and in our innocence we trusted the drop zone party to see fair

play 'between the gusts'. We were brought to the door a couple of times and watched dry-mouthed as the windsock strained in the breeze: finally, sense prevailed and the whole thing was called off. Later, David, who had been a parachutist in the Army, identified the sortie as a milestone for us both, 'At that moment,' he said with feeling. 'I stopped being just a parachutist and became a PJI.'

To use up fuel before landing our pilot circled at low level the nearby site where an identical aircraft to ours, a Hastings, had crashed during a PTS sortie: there had been no survivors.

That too was a milestone; an essential step in growing up as a PJI.

A most recognisable marker in PTS training history was laid down in July 1971 when the Prince of Wales, then undergoing flying training at the RAF College Cranwell, went to PTS to make a single parachute descent into the sea.

The School had a long-standing military commitment to 'water jump' training, chiefly for the Royal Marines, and George Sizeland's section prepared PJIs for that. It followed that what he proposed for the prince was no different to that for any other ab-initio trainee. Needless to say, for students of such eminence 'normality' proved difficult to maintain as George recalled:

I was told to report to the Officer Commanding PTS. He closed the door and in little more than a whisper told me that I had been selected to train a V.V.I.P. 'He is the most important VIP we have ever trained, but I can't tell you who it is' ... 'From now on you must only refer to him as Golden Falcon' ... This was the first of a series of meetings and very silly conversations involving people who had no idea of the history or role of PTS ...

George's place during the actual jump was on a Royal Marines' landing craft supervising drop zone safety in Studland Bay, just outside Poole Harbour. Despite the supposed secrecy, the event had become headline news in the *Daily Express*. To George's dismay every reader seemed to own a boat and had converged on Studland to see the fun:

Some were small and fast with photographers on board, some were larger and slower with the entire population of Dorset hanging over the side ...

As the aircraft approached George had been amazed to find a brigadier of Royal Marines in formal uniform – as was George – on board the craft. The senior officer justified his presence:

Well... it is my boat.

And, as the crowds pressed closer, he boosted George's confidence further:

I think we are going to have a few problems ...

The much-reported jump was routine despite a momentary snag in the parachute rigging lines and the day passed into PTS legend. It had been just another parachute task – perhaps – and Ken Kidd, the Prince's personal PJI, was ever after reported as advising his trainee: 'Better get a haircut, there's royalty about, you know.' Despite the triumphant conclusion, Sizeland remained convinced that inadvertent disclosure by him had alerted the hordes of sightseers to the 'secret' event:

I was very much concerned regarding the breach of security and felt that we were still under suspicion. After a week I phoned the security people. 'Don't worry about that, old boy,' they said. 'The Buckingham Palace press office pushed out a press release the night before and didn't bother to tell us.'

George Sizeland often quoted that task as a good example of PTS attracting attention from those who did not understand the School's ethos or, indeed anything associated with the black art of parachute training and jumping.

In April 1978 the Prince of Wales and Prince Andrew came to PTS, principally so that Prince Charles, the newly-appointed Colonel-in-Chief of the Parachute Regiment, could qualify as a military parachutist.

It was a busy period for those PJI's directly involved, but the work of PTS proceeded unhindered all around the 'Specials' course. The task and its outcome has been fully reported elsewhere, but, like George Sizeland seven years earlier, I seemed to spend a lot of time fighting off planning suggestions that only served to distract us from our primary purpose.

Thus, the 'Royal' training certainly became a personal milestone, but perhaps not a unit one; during the lead-up it became salutary to realise that some PJIs, serving away from PTS knew nothing whatever about our 'career highlight'.

Peter Hearn, almost off the RAF map at St Mawgan, near Newquay, didn't even know PTS was taking in the princes while Fred Marshal, to be appointed OC PTS in late 1979, only read of our exploits afterwards.

As an entirely unplanned and unofficial gesture, we persuaded Ken Kidd to take a day off (now civilian) work and, as Prince Charles bade farewell to PTS, stood him before his former pupil. Thus in accordance with parachuting tradition, even the Prince of Wales would not forget his first-jump PJI.

April 1989 saw my last parachute descent from a balloon. Terry Cooke and I jumped twice in quick succession onto an Aldershot drop zone littered with sharp, upwardly-pointing rugby posts. 'Better you than me,' quipped Ken D'Souza, the PJI despatcher, but then he knew he was not jumping that day. As a special treat, therefore, Terry 'volunteered' him to accompany me a couple of weeks later on my last jump ever.

The aircrew at Lyneham always needed 'jump fodder' to keep their flying procedure 'tick box' checks up to date, and, in the absence of Army parachutists, detachment PJIs would occasionally 'fill-in'– if only to maintain their own skills.

So, six if us went over to spend the day largely sitting around in a squadron crewroom while the aviators organised their sortie; at last, we got going by early afternoon.

'What,' I asked myself, standing in the open door with a deserted Salisbury Plain rolling past below, 'am I, in my 50th year, doing here? And are the old demons – anxiety, apprehension – still around?' Well, yes, they were, particularly anxiety; the day had gone on a bit, I had a long-standing date to meet with my wife that evening and the prospects of being on time were not good.

Ken D'Souza was unhappy too. He had just completed three years with the Falcons Display Team and all this low-level, ruffy-tuffy paratrooper stuff was definitely beyond the pale.

It took a long day to mount a six-man airborne assault, but it was a milestone.

Epilogue

A retirement date seemed a proper place to end this personal view of No 1 Parachute Training School and the Parachute Jumping Instructors – serving there or elsewhere. My direct involvement with the School ended in August 1989, but as my last posting required a PJI appointee, I retained distant contact until Summer 1993; having worn the badge with considerable pride for 27 years.

Despite recent shortages and the RAF transport fleet evidently having higher priority world-wide commitments, PTS continues in good heart and seemingly has absorbed its own 'milestones' without fuss. Two that readily come to mind are the end of parachuting from balloons in early 1995 and the arrival of fully-qualified and practising female PJIs.

The unit is still located at Brize Norton, making its 36-year life there the longest base location in the School's history. Command of the operational detachments to the Army and Royal Marines has devolved from direct PTS control to an RAF HQ function and then back again to a local PJI commander who includes the School in his remit.

Meeting the present-day generation of young PJIs at reunions is somewhat like stepping back in time; they are what we were: 30, 40, 50 years and more ago. We might be older, but wiser? Most PJIs' families would probably dispute that at times.

We are veterans – ancient cars bumbling down to Brighton? – we are the 'Old, Old Boys' now, but still have to defer on occasion to the real ones. Some travel considerable distances to reunions at PTS (and then have to be physically restrained from climbing 30ft into the hangar roof for a nostalgic leap off the Fan).

Today's parachute equipment and techniques might be unrecognisably sophisticated to us, but in a curious full-turn-of-the-wheel a modern low-level parachute is now cleared for the heights frantically sought in the heat of battle during World War II.

However, come what may, an essential certainty continues: young men (as I write, not yet women) are prepared to go to war by air and be delivered to the ground by parachute. Other young men and women have to train them to do that; having themselves been so trained.

There are rumbles in the undergrowth about the future of military parachuting: particularly so in late summer 2010 when a series of headlines declared that a hard-pressed RAF Hercules fleet was letting the Airborne side down. Variations on this theme have been around since the Ringway days, but in times of straightened military budgets rumours tend to carry more weight so it was nothing new to read a bleat that seemingly challenged the right of PTS to exist. Quoting a "Senior officer of the Parachute Regiment" a national broadsheet noted:

"The RAF retains an inordinate amount of control over military parachuting..."

In this context I interpret 'The RAF' as meaning PTS, and so claim that there is little in official correspondence, recorded and anecdotal history, or even crew room mythology to suggest that anything else would have served the British Airborne Forces better.

Perhaps the accounts in here have demonstrated that.

Neil Dawson, a modern young PJI wrote to the Canopy Club in summer 2006: he updated what we have all said over the years:

"Having had the honour of meeting and talking to past PJIs during Canopy Club reunions throughout my career, and listening to the extraordinary characters and their even more outlandish stories, I believe the bond or comparison between us lies with the people. Essentially we seem to be made of the same basic human elements ... the equipment, the political environment, the financial limitations may be different but the people, the characters remain the same

I have talked to many of today's PJIs who basically agree ... the job we do attracts a certain type of personality, which seems to be timeless and universal. The job may have changed, but in his or her essentials, PJIs remain the same."

In 2003 I ended my account of the Prince of Wales's training at PTS by noting that every time I then saw him, and any other airborne soldier in uniform, displaying parachute 'wings' I reminded myself:

"No 1 Parachute Training School saw to that."

It is a simple boast but worth repeating if only because of its essential truth.

Acknowledgements

Many of the words in here were written or spoken by former Parachute Jumping Instructors (PJIs) and have appeared in Canopy Club leaflets and newsletters. I am humbly grateful for their agreement to use them. Sadly, in the natural order of things, some of these men are no longer alive but my gratitude is no less appropriate. Any flaws in memory, interpretation and retrospective comment are mine alone.

As with most ex-service organisations, when PJI veterans meet they greet each other by name as friends and former comrades. With one or two exceptions I have followed that convention in this work and have not identified any PJI mentioned in the text by military rank. Personal thanks, therefore to:

Terry Allen, Dave Armstrong, Alan Brown, Alf Card, David Cobb, John Cole, Johnny Dawes, Neil Dawson, Gerry Delaney, Peter Denley, Bill Fell, Bill Forde, Danny Gavin, Kip Gilpin, Norman Goodacre, Geoff Greenland, Peter Hearn, Willie Hunter, Norman Hoffman, Alec Jackson, Bill Jevons, Wilf Jones, Peter Keane, Bob Kent, Ali MacDonald, Henry MacDonald, John Mace, Les Males, Grahame May, Roy McCluskey, Pete McCumiskey, Jake McLoughlin, Erroll Minter, Bryan Morris, Dick Mullins, Maurice Newnham, Ted Parks, Geordie Platts, George Podevin, Bob Roberts, John Robinson, Stan Roe, George Sizeland, Ron Smith, Bob Souter, Louis Strange, Chris Thorn, Peter Tingle, Val Valentine, Peter Watson, Harry Ward, Peter Williams & Jimmy Young.

More formal thanks to Group Captain P G Hearn AFC BA RAF(retd), President of the PTS Canopy Club (the association of Veteran PJIs) for permission to raid the Club journals and newsletters as well as delve into his own writings.

To successive Officers Commanding No1 Parachute Training School who have given me access to the unit archive over the years.

Thanks yet again to my old friend and former professional colleague, Squadron Leader George Sizeland MBE; a resolute curator of the unit's history.

I have been unable to trace any survivors of Sampson Low, Marston & Co Ltd who published the late Group Captain Maurice Newnham's authoritative account of the beginnings and subsequent wartime history of PTS: 'Prelude to Glory' (1947). My debt to them is considerable.

To Grub Street Publishing Ltd for permission to quote from 'Falcons' by Peter Hearn (1995).

To the British Limbless Ex-Servicemen's Association (BLESMA) for their agreement that the Canopy Club could use Danny Gavin's account of his early parachuting days.

And to all RAF Parachute Jumping Instructors with whom I served. I am sorry that everybody cannot feature in here, but thanks for the memories: it was a great 27years.

~ End ~